MW01092921

ARMENIAN FIRST NAMES

by

Nicholas Awde & Emanuela Losi

HIPPOCRENE BOOKS
NEW YORK

First Name Books from Hippocrene...

Arabic First Names
French First Names
Jewish First Names
Polish First Names
Spanish First Names

With thanks to Fred J. Hill & Hovann Simonian

Copyright © 2001 by Nicholas Awde & Emanuela Losi

All rights reserved.

Typeset & designed by Desert♥Hearts

ISBN 0 7818 0750 6

For information, address:
HIPPOCRENE BOOKS, INC.
171 Madison Avenue
New York, NY 10016
www.hippocrenebooks.com

Printed in the United States of America.

CONTENTS

A Note on Spelling

Armenian names across the world show great variety in their forms, not only because of the different systems of spelling found in the countries that use the Roman alphabet, but also because many of the names in this book are given in direct transliteration from the original Armenian. With a few exceptions, we have chosen the variants that use the pronunciation of Western Armenian, the majority language of the Diaspora.

An accent has been placed on the final -e of names where this letter should be pronounced, e.g. **Adriné** indicates its pronunciation is 'Ah-dree-nay.' This is for guidance only and is not intended as a rule of spelling.

The Armenian Alphabet					
Ա ա	a	Ծ ծ	dz (ts)	Ջ ջ	ch (j)
Բ բ	p (b)	Կ կ	g (k)	Ռ ռ	r
Գ գ	k (g)	Հ հ	h	Ս ս	s
Դ դ	t (d)	Ձ ձ	ts (dz)	Վ վ	v
Ե ե	e	Ղ ղ	gh	Տ տ	d (t)
Զ զ	z	Ճ ճ	j (ch)	Ր ր	r
Է է	e	Մ մ	m	Ց g	ts
Ը ը	ə/u	Յ յ	y/h	Ւ ւ	v
Թ թ	t	Ն ն	n	Փ փ	p
Ժ ժ	z/zh	Շ շ	sh	Ք ք	k
Ի ի	i	Ո ո	o	Օ o	o
Լ լ	l	Չ չ	j	Ֆ ֆ	f
Խ խ	kh	Պ պ	b (p)	Ու ու	ou/v

Letters in brackets represent Eastern Armenian variants.

4

ARMENIAN
GIRLS'
NAMES

A

Acho — Ա,չo
'The rightful one,' from the Armenian *ach* 'right hand.'

Adriné — Ա,տրինէ
'Adriatic maiden.' The English form of **Adrianne**,
a Latin name derived from the Adriatic Sea.
Alternative form: **Adrig** (Ա,տրիկ).

Aghavni — Ա,ղաւնի
'Dove,' from the Armenian.
Familiar form: **Aghounig** (Ա,ղունիկ), 'little dove.'
Aghvanie Zabel (1855-1920), artist in Constantinople.
Aghavni Haigazian (known as Siranoush; 1862-1932), Armenian classical stage actress.

Aghpiur — Ա,ղբիւր
'Fount,' from the Armenian.
Familiar form: **Aghpourig** (Ա,ղբուրիկ).

Aghvor — Ա,ղուոր
'Beautiful one,' from the Armenian.

Agner — Ա,կներ
'Jewels,' or 'beautiful eyes,' from the Armenian.

Agnesa — Ա,կնեսա
'Pure one,' from the Greek.
Alternative forms: **Agnes/Aknes** (Ա,կնէս).

7

Agourig — Ակուրիկ
'Little ax,' from the Armenian *agour* 'ax.'

Aida — Այտա
The name of the heroine of Giuseppi Verdi's
famous Italian opera that bears the same name.

Aidziam — Այծեմնիկ
'Young deer,' from the Armenian.
Familiar forms: **Aidzemnig** (Այծեմնիկ), and **Aidzig** (Այծիկ).

Aiki — Այգի
'Vineyard,' from the Armenian.

Aikoun — Այգուն
'Dawn,' from the Armenian.
Familiar form: **Aik** (Այգ).

Akabi — Ագապի
'Darling,' from the Greek.

Aknes — Ագնես
'Pure one,' from the Greek.
Alternative forms: **Agnes** (Ագնէս), and **Agnesa** (Ագնեսա).

Alenoush — Ալենոյշ
'Sweet ripple,' from the Armenian.

Alidz — Ալիծ
Alis — Ալիս
Alisa — Ալիսա
'One who always speaks the truth,' from the Greek.
The Armenian forms of **Alice** and **Alicia**.
Alicia Ghiragossian (1936-), award-winning Argentinian poet, later based in the U.S.

Alik — Ալիք
'Ripple,' from the Armenian.

Alin — Ալին
'Bearer of light,' from the Irish. The Armenian form of **Eileen**.
Alternative form: **Aliné** (Ալինէ).

Almasd — Ալմաստ
'Diamond,' from the Ottoman Turkish *almaz.*

Alvart — Ալվարդ
'Rose,' from the Arabic *al* 'the' and *ward* 'rose.'

Amalig — Ամալիկ
Amalya — Ամալիա
'Full of vitality,' from the name of a famous Ostrogoth family.

Anahid — Անահիտ
'Pure,' from the Armenian.
From the name of the Armenian goddess of the moon.
Alternative forms: **Anayis** (Անայիս), and **Ano** (Անո).

Angel — Անժէլ
'Angel,' from the Greek.
Alternative form: **Anzhel** (Անժէլ).
Familiar forms: **Angig/Anzhig** (Անժիկ).

Ani — Անի
The name of an ancient capital of Armenia.
Familiar forms: **Ania** (Անիա), and **Anig** (Անիկ).

Ankiné — Անգինէ
'Priceless,' from the Armenian.

Anna — Աննա
'Grace,' from the Hebrew.
Familiar form: **Annig** (Աննիկ).
Empress Anna, Armenian queen of Byzantium in the ninth century.
Anna Namourasian (known as Vartouhi; 1862-1945), Armenian comic actress.

Annuman — Աննման
'Unique,' from the Armenian.

Anoush — Անուշ
'Sweet,' from the Armenian, or 'immortal,' from the Pahlavi.
Familiar form: **Anoushig** (Անուշիկ).

Antaram — Անթարամ
'Evergreen,' from the Armenian.
Antaram de Trébizonde, title and heroine of a French novel by Paule Henry Bordeaux, published in Paris, 1930.

Antsrev — Անձրև
'Rain,' from the Armenian.
Familiar form: **Antsrevig** (Անձրևիկ).

Araksya — Արաքսիա
Arax — Արաքս
From Araks, the name of the national river of Armenia.
Alternative forms: **Araxi** (Արաքսի),
and **Araxia** (Արաքսիա).
Aracy Balabanian (1941-), award-winning Brazilian movie, television, and stage actress.

Arda — Արտա
An ancient name of unknown origin.
Princess Arda (11th century), the granddaughter of King Roupen I of Cilicia.

Ardanoush — Արտանույշ
'Maiden of Artvin,' a city in Western Armenia.

Ardemis — Արտեմիս
'Healthy,' from the Greek,
also the name of the Greek goddess of the moon.

Ardouyd — Արտույտ
'Skylark,' from the Armenian.

Ardzvi — Արծուի
Ardzvig — Արծուիկ
'Little eagle,' from the Armenian *ardziv* 'eagle.'

Areknazan — Արեգնազան
'Joy of the sun,' from the Armenian.
Familiar forms: **Arek** (Արեգ), and **Areknaz** (Արեգնազ).

Arev — Արեւ
'Sun,' from the Armenian.

Arevhad — Արեւհատ
'Spark of the sun,' from the Armenian *arev* 'sun' and *had* 'seed.'

Arevig — Արեւիկ
'Little sun,' from the Armenian.

Arlene — Արլին
'Pledge,' from the Celtic.
Arlene Francis (real name Arlene Kazanjian; 1908-), U.S. stage, movie, and television actress.

Armani — Արմանի
'Armenian girl,' from the Armenian.

Armanoush — Արմանոյշ
'Sweet Armenian girl,' from the Armenian.

Armaveni — Արմաւենի
'Date palm,' from the Armenian.

Armenia — Արմենիա
'Armenia,' from the Armenian.

Armenouh — Արմենուհի
'Armenian maiden,' from the Armenian.
Familiar form: **Armenig** (Արմենիկ).

11

Arminé — Արմինէ

The feminine form of Armen, dervived from Armaniag, the name of
the son of the Father of the Armenian people, Haig.
Familiar form: **Armig** (Արմիկ).

Arous — Արուս

'Bride,' from the Arabic *arus*;
or a short form of **Arousiag** (Արուսիակ).

Arousiag — Արուսիակ

'Venus,' or 'morning star,' from the Armenian.

Arpa — Արփա

The name of a river in Armenia.

Arpi — Արփի

'Sun,' from the Armenian.
Alternative forms: **Arpen** (Արփէն), and **Arpeni** (Արփենի).
Familiar forms: **Arpenig** (Արփենիկ), **Arpi** (Արփի), **Arpig** (Արփիկ),
Arpiné (Արփինէ), and **Arpo** (Արփo).

Arsenig — Արսենիկ

A familiar form of **Arsiné** (Արսինէ).

Arshaganoush — Արշականոյշ
Arshanoush — Արշանոյշ

'Sweet bear,' from the Armenian *arshag* 'bear,'
and *anoush* 'sweet.'
Alternative forms: **Arshig** (Արշիկ), and **Arsho** (Արշo).

Arshagouhi — Արշակուհի

'Bear maiden,' from the Armenian *arshag* 'bear.'

Arshalouys — Արշալույս

'Dawn,' from the Armenian.
Archalouïs Markarian (1914-), Armenian poet, born in Georgia and based in France.

Arsiné — Արսինէ
'Little woman,' from the Greek.
Familiar forms: **Arsenig** (Արսենիկ), and **Arshenig** (Արշենիկ).
Arsinée Khanjian (1958-), Canadian movie and television actress.

Asanet —Ասանէթ
'Calamity,' from the Hebrew *hasanet.*

Asdghig — Աստղիկ
'Little star.' The name of the ancient Armenian goddess of love.
Familiar forms: **Asdig** (Աստիկ), **Asghig** (Ասղիկ).

Ashkhen — Աշխէն
'Azure,' or 'blessed lady,' from the Armenian.
Queen Ashkhen (?-330), saint and martyr; the wife of King Drtad, martyr and the first monarch to convert to Christianity.

Ashnag — Աշննկ
The name of a village on the slopes of Mount Arakadz
and one of the rivers of Armenia.

Ashoun — Աշնուն
'Autumn,' from the Armenian.

Asler — Ասլեր
An ancient name of unknown origin.

Asli — Ասլի
'True,' from the Arabic.

Aslig — Ասլիկ
'Little apple,' from the Armenian.
Familiar form: **Aslin** (Ասլին).

Asmin — Ասմին
'Jasmine,' from the Armenian.

Astiné — Աստինէ
'Citizen,' from the Greek.

Azadouhi — Ազատուհի
'Free maiden,' from the Armenian.
Familiar forms: **Azadig** (Ազադիկ),
and **Azo** (Ազո).

Azkanoush — Ազգանուշ
'Sweet nation,' from the Armenian *azk* 'nation,'
and *anoush* 'sweet.'
Familiar forms: **Azkan** (Ազգան), and **Azkoush** (Ազգուշ).

Azniv — Ազնիւ
'Noble and gentle,' from the Armenian.
Azniv Hratchia (1853-1920), Armenian classical stage actress.

B

Baidzar — Պայծառ
'Brilliant,' from the Armenian.
Familiar forms: **Baidzig** (Պայծիկ), and **Baidzo** (Պայծո).

Bargeshd — Պարկեշտ
'Modest,' from the Armenian.

Barig — Պարիկ
'Nymph,' from the Armenian.

Barzanoush — Պարզանոյշ
'Sweet purity,' from the Armenian *barz* 'clean,' and *anoush* 'sweet.'

14

Barzig — Պարզիկ
'Pure,' from the Armenian *barz* 'clean.'

Beatris — Պէատրիս
'Joyful,' from the Latin.
The Armenian form of **Beatrice**.

Berjanoush — Պերճանոյշ
'Best and sweet,' from the Armenian *berj* 'best,'
and *anoush* 'sweet.'

Berjoug — Պերճուկ
Berjouhi — Պերճուհի
'Best maiden,' from the Armenian *berj* 'best.'
Familiar form: **Berjig** (**Պերճիկ**).

C

Cariné — Կարինէ
'Friend,' from the Armenian.

Cayané — Գայիանէ
'Joyful,' from the Latin *gaius*.

Chinar — Չինար
'Plane tree,' the sacred tree of ancient Armenia,
or 'artichoke,' from the Armenian

Cohar — Գոհար
'Jewel,' from the Persian/Arabic *jawhar*.
Familiar form: **Coharig** (**Գոհարիկ**).

D

Dadig — Տատիկ
'Little grandmother,' from the Armenian *dad* 'grandmother.'

Dajad — Տաճատ
Dajadouhi — Տաճատուհի
'Gift,' from the Classical Persian.
Dajad Antzevatsi, ninth-century commander of
the imperial army of Byzantium.

Datevig — Տաթեւիկ
From the name of the famous Armenian monastery of Datev.
Datevig Sazandarian (1916-), solo singer of the Yerevan Opera, Armenia.

Denchali — Տենչալի
'Desired,' from the Armenian.

Diana — Դիանա
The name of the Roman Goddess of the Moon
and protector of women.
Diana Der-Hovanessian, award-winning poet.

Dikoush — Դիգույշ
Dikranouhi — Դիգրանուհի
'Female warrior,' the feminine form of **Dikran** (Դիգրան).

Diroug — Տիրուկ
Dirouhi — Տիրուհի
'Princess,' from the Armenian.

Dirouni — Տիրունի
'Possessed,' from the Armenian.

Dzaghganoush — Ծաղկանուշ
'Sweet blossom,' from the Armenian.
Familiar form: **Dzaghgoush** (Ծաղկուշ).

Dzaghgasar — Ծաղկասար
'Mount of blossoms,' the name of a mountain in Armenia.

Dzaghgashad — Ծաղկաշատ
'Full of flowers,' from the Armenian.

Dzaghgashen — Ծաղկաշէն
'Created from flowers,' from the Armenian.

Dzaghginé — Ծաղկինէ
Dzaghig — Ծաղիկ
'Blossom,' from the Armenian *dzaghig* 'flower.'

Dzam — Ծամ
'The one with beautiful hair,' from the Armenian.
Familiar form: **Dzamig** (Ծամիկ).

Dzamer — Ծամեր
'Beautiful tresses,' from the Armenian *dzam* 'hair.'

Dzamosg — Ծամոսկի
'Golden-haired,' from the Armenian *dzam* 'hair,' and *vosgi* 'gold.'

Dzavig — Ծավիկ
'Little blue-eyed one,' from the Armenian *dzavi* 'blue.'

Dziadzan — Ծիածան
'Rainbow,' from the Armenian.
Alternative form: **Dzia** (Ծիա).

Dzidzar — Ծիծար
'Swift,' or 'swallow,' from the Armenian.

17

Dzotrin — Ʊnքրին
'Thyme,' from the Armenian.

Dzovach — Ʊավաչ
'Blue eyes,' from the Armenian.

Dzovan — Ʊnվան
Dzovig — Ʊnվիկ
'Sea maiden,' from the Armenian *dzov* 'sea.'

Dzovinar — Ʊnվինար
'Sea-born,' from the Armenian.
The name of the ancient Armenian goddess of the sky.
Dzovinar, mother of the heroes of Sassoun renowned for her dazzling beauty.

Է

Elena — Էլենա
'Flame,' from the Greek *elios* 'sun.'

Eliz — Էլիզ
Eliza — Էլիզա
Elo — Էլo
'Consecrated to God,' from the Hebrew.
The Armenian form of **Elizabeth**.

Eminé — Էմինէ
'Trustworthy woman,' from the Arabic *amin* 'safe.'

Emma — Էմմա
'Healer of the universe,' or 'woman who commands,'
from the Old Scandinavian.

Eva — Էւա
'Bearer of life,' from the Hebrew.

Eugenie — Էօժէնի
'Aristocratic,' from the Greek root *eu* 'good,' and *ghenos* 'family.'
Familiar form: **Eugig** (Էօժիկ).

F

Fenya — Ֆենիա
'Gift of God,' from the Russian/Greek name Fedosia.
Familiar form: **Fenig** (Ֆենիկ).

Fimi — Ֆիմի
'Lucky,' an alternative form of **Yevpimé**.

Firouz — Ֆիրուզ
'Victorious,' from the Persian.

G

Gadar — Կատար
'Peak,' from the Armenian.

Gagach — Կակաչ
'Poppy,' from the Armenian.

19

Gakav — Կաքաւ
'Partridge,' from the Armenian.
Familiar form: **Gakavig** (Կաքաւիկ).

Gamar — Կամար
'Arch,' or 'crescent,' from the Arabic *qamar* 'moon.'

Garab — Կարապ
'Swan,' from the Armenian.

Garin — Կարին
Gariné — Կարինէ
From the ancient name of the city of Erzroum,
in Western Armenia.

Gasia — Կասիա
'Cinnamon bush,' from the Armenian.

Gayané — Կայիանէ
'Joyful,' from the Latin *gaius*.
Alternative form: **Kayané** (Գայիանէ).
Gayané Khachturian (1942-), Armenian artist from Georgia.

Gitar — Կիթար
'Lute,' or 'guitar,' from the Armenian.
Familiar form: **Gitarig** (Կիթարիկ).

Glorig — Կլրիկ
'Curvaceous,' from the Armenian *glor* 'round.'

Gohag — Կոհակ
'Ripple,' from the Armenian.

Gousiné — Կուսինէ
'Maiden,' from the Armenian *gouys*. The Armenian form of **Virginia**.

H

Haghtouhi — Յաղթուհի
'Conquering woman,' from the Armenian.

Hagint — Յակինթ
'Hyacinth,' from the Armenian.

Haiganoush — Հայկանոյշ
'Sweet Armenian girl,' from the Armenian.
Alternative forms: **Haigan** (Հայկան), **Haigani** (Հայկանի),
and **Haigoush** (Հայկուշ).
Haiganoush Mark (1883-1966), journalist, writer, and defender of women's rights based in Istanbul.

Haigantoukhd — Հայկանդուխտ
'Daughter of Haig,' from the Armenian.
Familiar form: **Gantoukhd** (Կանդուխտ).

Haigoug — Հակուկ
Haigouhi — Հայկուհի
'Armenian girl,' from the Armenian.

Hainaz — Հայնազ
'Graceful Armenian,' from the Armenian.

Haivart — Հայվարդ
'Armenian rose,' from the Armenian.

Hamaspiur — Համասփիռ
'Campion flower,' from the Armenian.
Alternative form: **Hamas** (Համաս).

Hamazasbouhi — Համազասպուհի
'Possessing many horses,' from the Persian.

Hamegh — Համեղ
'Delicious,' from the Armenian.

Hamesd — Համեստ
Hamesdouhi — Համեստուհի
'Modesty,' from the Armenian.

Hasmig — Յասմիկ
'Jasmine,' from the Armenian.

Hasmig (Takouhi Hagopian; 1879-1947), Armenian comic actress.

Havad — Հաւատ
'Faith,' from the Armenian.

Haverj/Haverzh — Յաւերժ
'Eternal,' from the Armenian.

Haverjouhi — Յաւերժուհի
'Eternal woman,' from the Armenian.

Hayarpi — Հայարփի
'Armenian sun,' from the Armenian.

Hayasdan — Հայաստան
'Land of Armenia,' from the Armenian.

Hayots — Հայոց
'Armenian nation,' from the Armenian.

Hazarvart — Հազարվարդ
'Thousands of roses,' from the Persian *hazar* 'thousand'
and *vard* 'rose.'

Heghinar — Հեղինար
'Deer,' from the Armenian.

22

Heghiné — Հեղինէ
'Brilliant,' from the Greek. The Armenian form of **Helen**.
Empress Heghiné, wife of the first Byzantine Emperor Constantine I in the fourth century.
She found the relics of the True Cross of Jesus and ordered the building of
major churches in Jerusalem.

Heghnar — Հեղնար
'Deer,' from the Armenian.

Heghoush — Հեղուշ
An alternative form of **Heghiné** (Հեղինէ).

Hera — Հերա
From the name of the Greek goddess,
queen of the gods, and wife of Zeus.

Heranoush — Հերանուշ
'Flowing tresses,' from the Armenian.

Herik — Հերիք
'Capability,' from the Armenian.

Heriknaz — Հերիքնազ
'Enchanter,' from the Armenian.

Herminé — Հերմինէ
'Messenger,' from the Greek,
the feminine form of the Greek god Hermes.
Empress Herminé (919-961), wife of the Byzantine emperor Constantine VII.

Hezig — Հեզիկ
'Little friendly one,' from the Armenian *hez* 'friendly.'

Hmayel — Հմայել
'Charmer,' from the Armenian.

23

Hnazant — Հնազանդ
'Obedient,' from the Armenian.

Horompsimé — Հորոմփսիմէ
'Castaway,' from the Greek.

Horovel — Հորովել
'Chant of the plowman,' from the Armenian.

Houri — Հուրի
'Maiden of paradise,' or 'fire maiden,' from the Armenian.
Familiar form: **Hourig** (Հուրիկ); *see* **Hripsimé** (Հռիփսիմէ).

Housh — Յուշ
'Sweet memory,' from the Armenian.

Houshig — Յուշիկ
'Little memory,' or 'sweetly,' from the Armenian.

Hovanoush — Հովանուշ
'Sweet wind,' from the Armenian *hov* 'wind,' and *anoush* 'sweet.'

Hranoush — Հրանուշ
'Sweet fire,' from the Armenian *hour* 'fire,' and *anoush* 'sweet.'

Hrantouhi — Հրանդուհի
'Flame,' from the Armenian.

Hrarpi — Հրարփի
'Fire of the sun,' from the Armenian *hour* 'fire,' and *arpi* 'sun.'

Hratchouhi — Հրաչուհի
'Fiery eyes,' from the Armenian.

Hravart — Հրավարդ
'Fiery rose,' from the Armenian *hour* 'fire,' and *vart* 'rose.'

Hreghen — Հրեղէն
'Fiery,' from the Armenian.

Hripsimé — Հռիփսիմէ
'Cast away,' from the Greek.
Familiar forms: **Hourig** (Հուրիկ), and **Hrip** (Հռիփ).
Saint Hripsimé (265-301), nun and martyr.

I

Imasdouhi — Իմաստունի
'Wise woman,' from the Armenian.

Isgoug — Իսկուկ
Isgouhi — Իսկունի
'True queen,' from the Armenian.
Iskouhi Minas (1884-1974), Armenian novelist.

Ishkhanouhi — Իշխանունի
'Princess,' from the Armenian.

J

Jbid — Ժպիտ
'Smile,' from the Armenian.

Jemma — Ջեմմա
'Precious jewel,' from the Latin.

Jina — Զինա
'God's gracious gift,' from the Hebrew.

Joudig — Ջուտիկ
'Little chick,' from the Armenian *joud* 'chick.'

K

Kaghtsrig — Քաղցրիկ
'Little sweet one,' from the Armenian *kaghtsr* 'sweet.'

Kaghtsrouhi — Քաղցրուհի
'Sweet maiden,' from the Armenian *kaghtsr* 'sweet.'

Karoun — Գարուն
'Spring,' from the Armenian.

Kayané — Գայիանէ
'Joyful,' from the Latin *gaius*.
Alternative form: **Gayané** (Գայիանէ).
Saint Kayané (circa 265), nun and martyr.

Keghadzin — Գեղածին
'Born beautiful,' from the Armenian.

Keghani — Գեղանի
'Beautiful,' from the Armenian.

Keghanoush — Գեղանուշ
'Sweet beauty,' from the Armenian *keghetsig* 'beautiful,'
and *anoush* 'sweet.'
Familiar forms: **Keghoush** (Գեղուշ), and **Keghoushig** (Գեղուշիկ).

Keghashen — Գեղաշէն
'Beautifully formed,' from the Armenian.

Keghdzam — Գեղձամ
'Beautiful hair,' from the Armenian *keghetsig* 'beautiful,'
and *dzam* 'hair.'

Keghetsig — Գեղեծիկ
'Beautiful girl,' from the Armenian.
Alternative form: **Keghouhi** (Գեղուհի).

Kermanoush — Քրմանուշ
'Sweet high priestess,' from the Armenian.

Kermouhi — Քրմուհի
'High priestess,' from the Armenian.

Khachanoush — Խաչանուշ
'Sweet cross,' from the Armenian *khach* 'cross,' and *anoush* 'sweet.'

Khachouhi — Խաչուհի
'Maiden of the Cross,' from the Armenian *khach* 'cross.'

Khantoud — Խանդուտ
Khantout — Խանդուք
'Jealous in love,' from the Armenian.

Khatoun — Խաքուն
'Noble lady,' from the Ottoman Turkish.
Familiar form: **Khatounig** (Խաքունիկ).

Khngaper — Խնկաբեր
'Incense bearer,' from the Armenian.

Khngeni — Խնկենի
'Incense,' from the Armenian.

Khngig — Խնկիկ
'Sweet fragrance,' from the Armenian.

Khonarh — Խոնարհ
'Modesty,' from the Armenian.

Khosrovanoush — Խոսրովանուշ
'Sweet famous one,' from the Armenian *khosrov* 'famous,'
and *anoush* 'sweet.'

Khosrovitoukhd — Խոսրովիդուխտ
'Daughter of renown,' from the Armenian *khosrov* 'famous.'
and Persian *dokhtar* 'daughter.'
*Princess Khosrovitoukht (?-330), saint and martyr; the daughter of King Drtad,
martyr and first monarch to convert to Christianity.*

Kinevart — Գինեվարդ
'Rose wine,' from the Armenian *kine* 'wine,' and *vart* 'rose.'

Kisag — Գիսակ
'Long haired,' from the Armenian.

Klkhatir — Գլխադիր
'Veil,' from the Armenian.

Knar — Քնար
'Harp,' from the Armenian.
Familiar form: **Knarig** (Քնարիկ).

Knkoush — Քնքուշ
'Dainty,' from the Armenian.

Kohar — Գոհար
'Jewel,' from the Persian/Arabic *jawhar*.
Familiar form: **Koharig** (Գոհարիկ).
Kohar Kasparian (1924-), Armenian popular singer.

L

Lachag — Լաչակ
'Veil,' from the Armenian.

Lala — Լալա
'Tulip,' from the Persian *lale*.
Alternative forms: **Lalé** (Լալէ), and **Lalig** (Լալիկ).

Lalazar — Լալազար
'Lotus,' from the Persian.

Lalvar — Լալվար
'Grapevine,' from the Armenian.

Lar — Լար
Lara — Լարա
Larisa — Լարիսա
'Joyous maiden,' from the Greek.

Lazour — Լազուր
'Azure,' from the Arabic, or 'helped by God,' from the Hebrew.

Leia — Լեյա
Lia — Լիա
'Inquistive,' from the Hebrew *le'ah*.

Lena — Լենա
'Charmer,' a short form of the Latin **Magdalen**.

Lernouhi — Լեռնուհի
'Maiden of the mountains,' from the Armenian
ler 'mountain.'

29

Liasdan — Լիասդան
'Land of riches,' from the Armenian.

Lilia — Լիլիա
Lilian — Լիլիան
Lilig — Լիլիկ
Lily — Լիլի
'Lily,' from the Latin.

Lilipar — Լիլիփար
'Tulip bearer,' from the Persian.

Lor — Լոր
Lora — Լորա
'Pretty,' from the Armenian.
Familiar form: Lori (Լորի).

Lori — Լորի
'Maiden of Lori,' a region of Armenia.

Lorig — Լորիկ
'Little pretty one,' from the Armenian.

Louiza/Luiza — Լուիզա
'Warrior maiden,' from the Old Germanic.

Lousadzin — Լուսածին
'Born of light,' from the Armenian *louys* 'light.'

Lousaher — Լուսահեր
'Shining-haired,' from the Armenian.

Lousakegh — Լուսագեղ
'Illuminated,' from the Armenian.

Lousanna — Լուսաննա
'Shining Anna,' from the Armenian.

Lousanoush — Լուսանուշ
'Sweet light,' from the Armenian *louys* 'light,' and *anoush* 'sweet.'

Lousaper — Լուսապեր
'Bringer of light,' from the Armenian.
Alternative forms: **Lousap** (Լուսապ), **Lous** (Լուս), and **Louso** (Լուսո).

Lousarad — Լուսարատ
'Filled with light,' from the Armenian.

Lousarpi — Լուսարփի
'Shining sun,' from the Armenian.

Lousatsor — Լուսածոր
'Valley of light,' from the name of a river in Armenia.

Louseghen — Լուսեղէն
'Bright,' from the Armenian.
Alternative form: **Lousashogh** (Լուսաշող), 'radiant.'

Louseres — Լուսերես
'Shining-faced,' from the Armenian.

Lousia — Լուսիա
'Maiden of light,' from the Armenian *louys* 'light.'

Lousin — Լուսին
Lousiné — Լուսինէ
Lousnag — Լուսնակ
'Moon,' from the Armenian.
Familiar form: **Lousig** (Լուսիկ).
Lousig Sargavak, *19th-century grammarian.*
Lucine Amarda, *20th-century U.S. classical singer.*
Lousiné Zakarian (1937-1993), *soloist singer of the Yerevan Opera, Armenia.*

Lousntak — Լուսնթագ
'Jupiter,' from the Armenian.

Lousvart — Լուսվարդ
'Bright rose,' from the Armenian *louys* 'light,' and *vart* 'rose.'

Luci — Լուսի
Lucia — Լուսիա
'Bearer of light,' from the Latin.
The Armenian form of **Lucy**.

Madlen — Մատլէն
Magda — Մակտա
'Woman of strength and courage,' from the Greek.
An Armenian form of **Magdalene**.

Maida — Մայտա
'Maiden,' from the English.

Mairanoush — Մայրանուշ
'Sweet mother,' from the Armenian *mair* 'mother,'
and *anoush* 'sweet.'

Maireni — Մայրենի
Mairiné — Մայրինէ
'Mother,' from the Armenian *mair* 'mother.'

Makaghat — Մագաղաթ
'Scroll,' from the Armenian.

Makhmour — Մախմուր
'Velvet,' from the Ottoman Turkish.

Mako — Մաֆo
An alternative form of **Makrouhi**.

Makour — Մաֆուր
'Pure,' from the Armenian.

Makriné — Մագրինէ
'Purity,' from the Armenian *makour* 'pure.'
Familar form: **Makoush** (Մաֆուշ).

Makrouhi — Մաֆրուհի
'Pure maiden,' from the Armenian *makour* 'clean.'
Familiar form: **Makroun** (Մաֆրունֆ).

Maktaghiné — Մագդաղինէ
'Woman of strength and courage,' from the Greek.
The Armenian form of **Magdalene**.

Mamé — Մամէ
'Mother,' from the Armenian.
Familiar form: **Mamig** (Մամիկ).

Mané — Մանէ
'Fern,' from the Armenian.
Familiar forms: **Mania** (Մանիա), **Manni** (Մաննի),
and **Mannig** (Մաննիկ).
Saint Mané (circa 320), nun and hermit.

Mangouhi — Մանկուհի
'Little maiden,' from the Armenian.

Maniag — Մանիակ
'Necklace,' from the Armenian.

Manishag — Մանիշակ
Manoushag — Մանուշակ
'Violet,' from the Armenian.
Alternative forms: **Manish** (Մանիշ), and **Manoush** (Մանուշ).

Maral — Մարալ
'Beautiful deer,' from the Armenian.

Marchan — Մարջան
'Coral,' or 'red coral,' from the Armenian.
Familiar form: **Marchig** (Մարչիկ).

Maria — Մարիա
'Lady,' from the Hebrew.
Familiar forms: **Mara** (Մարա), **Mari** (Մարի),
Marieta (Մարիետա), and **Maro** (Մարո).
Maro Markarian (1915-), Armenian poet.

Mariam — Մարիամ
'Sea drop,' from the Hebrew *mar* 'drop,' and *yam* 'sea';
or 'princess,' from the Ancient Egyptian.
Alternative form: **Maroush** (Մարուշ).
Familiar form: **Maremig** (Մարեմիկ).

Mariné — Մարինէ
'Sea maiden,' from the Italian.
Familiar form: **Mara** (Մարա).

Marinoush — Մարինուշ
'Sweet Mary,' from **Mari**, and *anoush* 'sweet.'

Marits — Մարից
Maritsa — Մարիցա
'Born of the sea,' from the Latin.

Markaré — Մարգարէ
Markarid — Մարգրիտ
'Daisy.' The Armenian form of **Margaret**.
Alternative forms: **Markar** (Մարգար), and **Marko** (Մարգո).
Familiar form: **Markoush** (Մարգուշ).

Marmar — Մարմար
'Marble,' from the Armenian.

Marta — Մարթա
'Mistress,' from the Armenian.
The Armenian form of **Martha**.

Masour — Մասուր
'Dogrose berry,' from the Armenian.

Masreni — Մասրենի
'Dogrose blossom,' from the Armenian.

Matild — Մաթիլտ
'Valorous warrior maiden,' from the Old Germanic *maht* 'force,'
and *hilta* 'battle.'

Mayis — Մայիս
'May,' from the Armenian.

Meghag — Մեղակ
'Clove,' from the Armenian.

Megheti — Մեղեդի
'Melody,' from the Armenian.

Meghranoush — Մեղրանուշ
'Sweet honey,' from the Armenian *meghr* 'honey,'
and *anoush* 'sweet.'
Alternative form: **Meghoush** (Մեղուշ).

Meghrig — Մեղրիկ
'Little honey,' from the Armenian *meghr* 'honey.'

Mehrouhi — Մեհրուհի
'Sun maiden,' from the Armenian.

35

Melani — Մելանի
Melania — Մելանիա
Meliné — Մելինէ
'Dark one,' from the Greek.
Alternative form: **Melo** (Մելո).

Melanoush — Մելանուշ
'Pretty one,' from the Armenian.

Menig — Մենիկ
'Matchless daughter,' from the Armenian.

Mentouhi — Մենդուհի
An ancient name of unknown origin.
Alternative form: **Mentoug** (Մենդուկ).

Metaxia — Մեդաքսիա
'Silk,' from the Greek.
Metaxia Simonian (1926-1987), Armenian stage and movie actress.

Mihranoush — Միհրանուշ
'Sweet gift of the sun,' from the Armenian.

Mikanoush — Միգանուշ
'Sweet mist,' from the Armenian *mek* 'mist,' and *anoush* 'sweet.'

Miranoush — Միրանուշ
'Sweet gift of the sun,' from the Armenian.

Ո

Nairi/Nayiri — Նայիրի
'River,' or 'land of canyons,' from one of the ancient
names of Armenia.
Alternative forms: **Naira** (Նաիրա), **Nairé** (Նաիրէ),
Niri (Նիրի), and **Nirig** (Նիրիկ).
Nairi Zarian (1900-1969), Armenian poet, novelist, and playwright.

Nakhshoun — Նախշուն
'Fair and freckled,' from the Armenian.

Nan — Նան
Nana — Նանա
Nané — Նանէ
'Mother of all mothers,' from the ancient Armenian goddess Nana.
Alternative forms: **Naner** (Նաներ), **Nani** (Նանի),
and **Nanor** (Նանոր).
Familiar forms: **Nanig** (Նանիկ), and **Nanoush** (Նանուշ).

Naré — Նարէ
'Flame,' from the Arabic *nar* 'fire.'

Nargiz — Նարկիզ
'Narcissus,' from the Persian *nargis* 'narcissus flower.'

Narin — Նարին
Nariné — Նարինէ
'Fiery,' from the Arabic/Persian *nar* 'fire.'
Alternative form: **Nara** (Նարա).

Narod — Նարոտ
'Wedding ribbon,' from the Armenian.

Naz — Նազ
'Little enchanter,' from the Armenian.
Familiar forms: **Nazoud** (Նազուտ), and **Nazoug** (Նազուկ).

Nazani — Նազանի
'Enchanting one,' from the Armenian.
Alternative forms: **Nazan** (Նազան), **Nazé** (Նազէ),
and **Nazeli** (Նազելի).

Nazanig — Նազանիկ
'Little enchanting one,' from the Armenian.
Familiar form: **Nazig** (Նազիկ).

Nazlou — Նազլու
'Enchanting,' from the Ottoman Turkish.

Negdar — Նեկտար
'Nectar,' from the Armenian.

Nevrig — Նեվրիկ
An ancient name of unknown origin.

Nigoush — Նիկուշ
'Victory of the people,' from the Greek root
nike 'victory,' and *laos* 'people.'
The Armenian form of **Nicole**.

Nirva — Նիրվա
'Eternal bliss,' from the Sanskrit *nirvana*.

Nono — Նոնո
'Little shining one,' from the Armenian.
Alternative forms: **Nourig** (Նուրիկ), and **Nouritsa** (Նուրիծա).

Nora — Նորա
'God is my Light,' from the Greek.

Nouné — Նունէ

'Purified,' from the Assyrian.
Familiar form: **Nouno** (Նունo).
Saint Nouné (or Nino; ?-320), nun who converted the neighboring kingdom of Georgia to Christianity.
Nonny Hogrogian (1932-), award-winning American illustrator.

Nounig — Նունիկ

'Little purified one,' from the Armenian.

Nounoufar — Նունուֆար

'Waterlily,' from the Persian.

Nouritsa — Նուրիցա

'Shining,' from the Arabic *nur* 'shining.'

Noushig — Նուշիկ

'Little almond,' from the Armenian *noush* 'almond.'

Noyemi — Նոյեմի

'My darling,' from the Hebrew.
Alternative form: **Noyem** (Նոյեմ).

Noyemig — Նոյեմիկ

'My little darling,' from the Hebrew.

Noyemzar — Նոյեմզար

The name of the wife of the Prophet Noah.
Alternative form: **Nemzar** (Նեմզար).

Nvart — Նուարդ

'New rose,' from the Armenian.
Asbed Nevart (1900-1923), Armenian poet.

Nver — Նուէր

'Gift,' from the Armenian.

O

Ogher — Օղեր
'Earrings,' from the Armenian *ogh*.
Familiar form: **Oghig** (Օղիկ).

Olga — Օլգա
'Saintly,' from the Russian.

Orig — Օրիկ
'Sweet day,' from the Armenian *or* 'day.'

Oror — Օրոր
'Lullaby,' from the Armenian.

Ovsanna — Օվսաննա
'Praise,' from the Hebrew *hosanna*.
Alternative forms: **Osan** (Օսան), **Osig** (Օսիկ), and **Ovsan** (Օվսան).

P

Pailadzou — Փայլածու
'Mercury,' from the Armenian.

Pailanoush — Փայլանուշ
'Sweet shining light,' from the Armenian *pail* 'shine,'
and *anoush* 'sweet.'

Pailig — Փայլիկ
'Little shining light,' from the Armenian *pail* 'to shine.'

40

Pailiné — Փայլինէ
'Shining light,' from the Armenian *pail* 'to shine.'

Pailoun — Փայլուն
'Shining,' from the Armenian.

Palasan — Բալասան
'Balsam,' from the Armenian.
Alternative forms: Pala (Բալա), Palas (Բալաս),
and Palo (Բալo).

Palig — Բալիկ
'Little child,' from the Armenian *pala*.

Parantsem —Փառանձեմ
'Glory,' from the Armenian.
Alternative form: Paro (Փառo).
Queen Parantsem (fourth century), wife of King Arshag II, renowned
for her great beauty.

Pardi — Բարտի
'Sapling,' from the Armenian.

Pareli — Փարելի
'Lovely,' from the Armenian.

Pari — Բարի
'Kind,' from the Armenian.

Parig — Բարիկ
'Little glory,' from the Armenian.

Parkouhi — Փառքուհի
'Maiden of glory,' from the Armenian.

Parouhi — Բարուհի
'Sweet maiden,' from the Armenian *pari*.

Patig — Բաթիկ
'Duckling,' from the Armenian *pat* 'duck.'

Patil — Փաթիլ
'Snowflake,' from the Armenian.

Pavagan — Բավական
'Satisfaction,' from the Armenian.
Alternative form: **Pavaganouhi** (Բավականուհի).

Pebroné — Փեբրոնէ
An ancient name from the Greek.

Pehez — Բեհեզ
'Muslin,' from the Armenian.

Pergrouhi — Բերկրուհի
Pergroush — Բերկրուշ
'Delight,' from the Armenian.

Peri — Փերի
'Fairy,' from the Armenian.

Perouz — Փերուզ
'Jewel,' from the Persian.
Perouz, 19th- and 20th-century actress who starred in the theaters of Constantinople.

Persap — Բերսապ
Persapé — Բերսապէ
'Primrose,' or 'prize,' from the Armenian.
Familiar form: **Persig** (Բերսիկ).

Pirouz — Փիրուզ
'Jewel,' from the Persian.

Piunig — Փիւնիկ
'Phoenix,' from the Armenian.

Plpoul — Բլբուլ
'Nightingale,' from the Armenian.

Pnchig — Փնջիկ
'Little bouquet,' from the Armenian.

Poulig — Բուլիկ
'Little shrub,' from the Armenian.

Pounig — Բունիկ
'Little nest,' from the Armenian.

Pourasdan — Բուրաստան
'Flower garden,' from the Armenian.
Familiar forms: **Pourig** (Բուրիկ),
and **Pouro** (Բուրօ).

Pouys — Բոյս
'Herb,' from the Armenian.
Familiar form: Pousig (Բուսիկ).

Prapion — Բրաբիոն
'Primrose,' or 'prize,' from the Armenian.

Punig — Փունիկ
'Phoenix,' from the Armenian.

Puragn — Բիւրակն
'Thousand fountains,' from the Armenian.

Puregh — Բիւրեղ
'Crystal,' from the Armenian.

Puzantouhi — Բիւզադուհի
'Byzantine maiden,' from the Armenian.

R

Razmouhi — Ռազմուհի
'Warrior maiden,' from the Armenian.

Rehan — Ռեհան
'Sweet basil,' from the Armenian.

Repega — Ռեբեկա
'Bond,' from the Hebrew — signifies a woman who holds on to her man through her virtues. The Armenian form of **Rebecca**.

Roza — Ռոզա
'Rose,' from the Latin.

S

Sahaganoush — Սահականուշ
The feminine form of **Sahag**, from the Hebrew 'he laughs.'
Queen Sahaganoush (fifth century), saintly wife of Saint Sahag, and mother of Saint Shoushan.

Salpi — Սալբի
'Cypress,' from the Armenian.

Sanahin — Սանահին
From the name of a famous Armenian monastery.

Santoukhd — Սանդուխտ
'Dear daughter,' from the Persian.
Saint Santoukhd the Virgin Princess (75-110), noblewoman who was the first witness for Christianity in Armenia.

Sara — Սառա
'Princess,' from the Hebrew.

Sarig — Սարիկ
'Blackbird,' or 'little mountain,' from the Armenian.

Sarin — Սարին
'Mountain rmaiden,' from the Armenian.

Satenig — Սաթենիկ
Satig — Սաթիկ
Satiné — Սաթինէ
'Little amber,' from the Armenian *sat* 'amber.'
Familiar forms: **Saten** (Սաթէն), and **Sato** (Սաթօ).
Queen Satenig, queen of Ancient Armenia.

Seda — Սեդա
'Spirit of the forest,' from the Armenian.

Ser — Սէր
'Love,' from the Armenian.
Familiar form: **Sirig** (Սիրիկ)

Serig — Սէրիկ
A petname for **Ser** (Սէր).

Seta — Սեղա
'Lady,' from the Arabic *sayyida*.

Sevachia — Սեւաչեայ
'Dark-eyes,' from the Armenian.

45

Sevan — Սեվան
The name of a lake in Armenia.

Sevlig — Սեվլիկ
'Little dark one,' from the Armenian.

Sevoug — Սեվուկ
'Dark one,' from the Armenian.

Seyranouhi — Սէյրանուհի
'Sweet leisure,' from the Arabic.

Shaghosgi — Շաղոսկի
'Golden dew,' from the Armenian *shagh* 'dew,' and *vosgi* 'gold.'
Familiar forms: **Shaghig** (Շաղիկ), and **Shaghiné** (Շաղինէ).

Shahantoukhd — Շահանդուխտ
'Princess,' from the Persian *shah* 'king,'
and *dokhtar* 'daughter.'

Shahnaz — Շահնազ
'Enchanter of the king,' from the Armenian/Persian.

Shahosgi — Շահոսկի
'Royal gold,' from the Armenian *shah* 'king,' and *vosgi* 'gold.'

Shakar — Շաքար
'Sugar,' from the Armenian.

Shaké — Շաքէ
An ancient name of unknown origin.

Shamam — Շամամ
'Sweet melon,' from the Armenian.
Familiar forms: **Shami** (Շամի), and **Shamig** (Շամիկ).

Shamiram — Շամիրամ
'Zenith,' from the Armenian.

Sharmagh — Շարմաղ
'Fair of face,' from the Armenian.

Shnorhig — Շնորհիկ
'Graceful one,' from the Armenian.

Shoghag — Շողակ
Shoghagat — Շողակաթ
'Radiance,' from the Armenian *shogh* 'ray.'

Shogher — Շողեր
'Rays of light,' from the Armenian *shogh* 'ray.'

Shoghig — Շողիկ
'Little ray of light,' from the Armenian *shogh* 'ray.'

Shoushan — Շուշան
Shoushiné — Շուշինէ
'Lily,' from the Armenian.
Saint Shoushan (circa 470), saint and martyr.

Shoushanig — Շուշանիկ
Shoushig — Շուշիկ
'Little lily,' from the Armenian.
Shoushanig Kourghinian (1876-1927), Armenian poet.

Sibil — Սիպիլ
The name of a legendary prophetess from Ancient Greece.
Sibyl (real name Zabel Asadour; 1863-1934), poet, novelist, and defender of women's rights, based in Constantinople.

Silva — Սիլվա
'Forest maiden,' from the Latin.
Alternative forms: Silvi (Սիլվի), and Silvia (Սիլվիա).
Silva Gaboudikian (1919-), Armenian writer and poet.

Siramark — Սիրամարգ
'Peacock,' from the Armenian.
Alternative forms: **Sina** (Սինա), **Sinam** (Սինամ), and **Sira** (Սիրա).

Siranoush — Սիրանուշ
'Sweet love,' from the Armenian *ser* 'love,' and *anoush* 'sweet.'
Alternative forms: **Siran** (Սիրան),
and **Siroush** (Սիրուշ).
Siranoush (real name Aghavni Haigazian; 1862-1932), Armenian classical stage actress.

Sirarpi — Սիրարփի
'Love of the sun,' from the Armenian *ser* 'love,' and *arpi* 'sun.'
Sirarpi Der-Nersessian (1896-1989), Armenian art historian.

Sirazart — Սիրազարդ
'Ornament of love,' from the Armenian.

Sireli — Սիրելի
'Sweetheart,' from the Armenian.

Sirig — Սիրիկ
A familiar form of **Ser** (Սեր).

Siroug — Սիրուկ
Sirouhi — Սիրուհի
'Sweetheart,' from the Armenian.

Siroun — Սիրուն
'Lovely,' from the Armenian.

Sirvart — Սիրվարդ
'Rose of love,' from the Armenian.

Sis — Սիս
The name of the capital of the Armenian
kingdom of Cilicia.
Alternative form: **Sisvan** (Սիսվան).

Sisvart — Սիսվարդ
'Rose of Sis,' from Sis, and *vart* 'rose.'

Soghomé — Սողոմէ
'Peacemaker,' the feminine form of **Soghomon**.

Sokhag — Սոխակ
'Nightingale,' from the Armenian.

Sona — Սոնա
'Statuesque,' from the Armenian.

Sonia — Սոնիա
'Wise one,' from the Greek.
Familiar form: **Sonig** (Սոնիկ).

Sosé — Սոսէ
Sosi — Սոսի
'Plane tree,' the sacred tree of Ancient Armenia.
Familiar form: **Sosig** (Սոսիկ).

Sousam — Սուսամ
'Sesame,' from the Armenian.

Sousampar – Սուսամբար
'Sweet marjoram,' from the Armenian.
Alternative form: **Souso** (Սուսո).

Sousan — Սուսան
'Lily,' from the Hebrew *shushan*.
The Armenian form of **Susan**.

Sousanna — Սուսաննա
'Lily,' from the Hebrew *shushan*.
The Armenian form of **Suzanna**.

Srpig — Սրփիկ
Srpoug — Սրբուկ
Srpouhi — Սրբուհի
Srpoun — Սրբուն
'Holy woman,' from the Armenian.
Serpouhi Dussab (1842-1901), writer, poet and humanitarian.

Տ

Takosgi — Թագոսկի
'Crowned with gold,' from the Armenian *tak* 'crown,' and *vosgi* 'gold.'

Takouhi — Թագուհի
'Queen,' from the Armenian.
Alternative forms: Tako (Թագօ), Takoug (Թագուկ),
and Takoush (Թագուշ).
Takouhi Hagopian (known as Hasmig; 1879-1947), Armenian comic actress.

Takoun — Թաքուն
'Secret,' from the Armenian.

Talar — Դալար
'Verdant,' from the Armenian.
Familiar forms: Talarig (Դալարիկ), and Tali (Դալի).

Talin — Թալին
The name of a town and its surrounding region in Armenia.

Tamar — Թամար
Tamara — Թամարա
'Date fruit,' from the Hebrew.

Tangakin — Թանկագին
'Precious,' from the Armenian *tang* 'expensive.'

Tanganoush — Թանկանուշ
'Sweet precious maiden,' from the Armenian *tang* 'expensive,' and *anoush* 'sweet.'

Tangig — Թանկիկ
'Little precious maiden,' from the Armenian *tang* 'expensive.'

Tarouhi — Դարուհի
'Century,' from the Armenian *tar* 'century.'

Teghtsan — Դեղձան
'Blonde,' from the Armenian.

Teghtsanig — Դեղձանիկ
Teghtsig — Դեղձիկ
'Canary,' from the Armenian.

Teghtsoughi — Դեղձուհի
'Little peach,' from the Armenian *teghts* 'peach.'
Alternative form: Teghtso (Դեղձո).

Titar — Թիթառ
Titer — Թիթեռ
'Butterfly,' from the Armenian *titernig*.

Titsanoush — Դիցանուշ
Titsouhi — Դիցուհի
'Goddess,' from the Armenian.

Tokhig — Դոխիկ
'Dove,' from the Armenian.

Toukhdzam — Թուխձամ
'Raven-haired,' from the Armenian *toukh* 'dark,' and *dzam* 'hair.'

51

Toukhig — Թուխիկ
'Little dark one,' from the Armenian *toukh* 'dark.'

Toushig — Թուշիկ
'Little cheek,' from the Armenian *toush* 'cheek.'

Toutag — Թութակ
'Parrot,' from the Armenian.
Familiar forms: **Toutig** (Թութիկ), and **Touto** (Թութօ).

Trchnag — Թռչնակ
'Little bird,' from the Armenian.

Trvanda — Թրվանդա
'New fruit,' from the Armenian.

Tsainig — Ձայնիկ
'Little voice,' from the Armenian *tsain* 'voice.'

Tsdrig — Դստրիկ
'Little daughter,' from the Armenian *tousdr* 'daughter.'

Tshkho — Դշխոյ
'Queen,' from the Armenian.
Alternative forms: **Tshkhouhi** (Դշխուհի), and **Tshkhoun** (Դշխուն).

Tsndzaghig — Ձնծաղիկ
'Spring snowflake,' from the Armenian.

Tsoghig — Ցօղիկ
'Morning dew,' from the Armenian.

Tsoler — Ցոլեր
'Reflections,' from the Armenian *tsol* 'reflection.'
Alternative form: **Tsoliné** (Ցոլինէ)

Tsvig — Ձուիկ
'Little egg,' from the Armenian.

U

Ughtsanoush — Ուղձանուշ
'Fairy,' from the Armenian *ughts* 'wish,' and *anoush* 'sweet.'

Undza — Ընծայ
'Gift,' from the Armenian.

Untsag — Ընձակ
'Tiger cub,' from the Armenian.

Untsanoush — Ընձանուշ
'Sweet tiger cub,' from the Armenian *untsag* 'tiger cub,'
and *anoush* 'sweet.'

V

Vahantoukhd — Վահանդուխտ
'Daughter of Vahan,' from the Armenian god of war Vahan, and
toukhd 'daughter.'

Vana — Վանա
'Maiden from Van,' a city in Western Armenia.
Familiar form: **Vanig** (Վանիկ).

Vanda — Վանտա
'Water nymph,' from the Teutonic.

Vané — Վանէ
Vaneni — Վանենի
'Crystal,' from the Armenian.
Alternative form: **Vanya** (Վանիա).

Vanouhi — Վանուհի
Vanoush — Վանուշ
'Maiden from Van,' a city in Western Armenia.

Varaztoukhd — Վարազդուխտ
'Daughter of wild boar,' from the Persian *varaz* 'wild boar,'
and *dokhtar* 'daughter.'
Alternative form: **Vara** (Վարա).

Varoujnag/Varouzhnag — Վարուժնակ
'Turtledove,' from the Armenian.

Varsenig — Վարսենիկ
'Beautiful hair,' from the Armenian *vars* 'hair.'
Familiar form: **Varsig** (Վարսիկ).

Varser — Վարսեր
'Beautiful tresses,' from the Armenian *vars* 'hair.'

Vart — Վարդ
'Rose,' from the Armenian.

Vartanoush — Վարդանուշ
'Sweet rose,' from the Armenian *vart* 'rose,' and *anoush* 'sweet.'

Vartehad — Վարդեհատ
'Roseberry,' from the Armenian *vart* 'rose,' and *hadig* 'berry.'

Varteni — Վարդենի
Vartiné — Վարդինէ
'Rose-bush,' from the Armenian.

Varter — Վարդեր
'Roses,' from the Armenian *vart* 'rose.'

Varteres — Վարդերես
'Rosy cheeked,' from the Armenian.

Varti — Վարդի
Vartig — Վարդիկ
'Little rose,' from the Armenian.

Vartishagh — Վարդիշաղ
'Rose dew,' from the Armenian.

Vartiter — Վարդիթեր
'Rose petal,' from the Armenian.

Varto — Վարդo
'Rose,' from the Armenian.

Vartoug — Վարդուկ
Vartouhi — Վարդուհի
Vartoush — Վարդուշ
'Rose maiden,' from the Armenian.
Vartouhi (real name Anna Namourasian; 1862-1945),
Armenian comic actress.

Vazkanoush — Վազգանուշ
'Sweet frog,' from the Persian.
Alternative form: Vazkoush (Վազգուշ).

Vazkenouhi — Վազգենուհի
'Frog maiden,' from the Persian.

Vehan — Վեհան
Vehiné — Վեհինէ
'Royal one,' from the Armenian *veh* 'royal.'

Vehanoush — Վեհանուշ
'Sweet royal one,' from the Armenian *veh* 'royal,' and *anoush* 'sweet.'
Familiar form: Vehig (Վեհիկ).

Verchalouys — Վերջալոյս
'Dusk,' from the Armenian.

Vera — Վերա
'True,' from the Latin. It also has the Russian meaning of 'faith.'

Vergin/Verzhin — Վերժին
Verkin — Վերգին
Verkiné — Վերգինէ
'Pure maiden,' from the French/Latin. The Armenian form of **Virginia**.
Familiar forms: Vergig/Verzhig (Վերժիկ),
and Verkoush (Վերգուշ).

Viktoria — Վիքթորիա
'Victory,' from the Latin.

Vokouhi — Ոգուհի
'Spirit maiden,' from the Armenian *voki* 'spirit.'

Vosgebar — Ոսկեպար
'Golden dance,' from the Armenian.

Vosgedzam — Ոսկեծամ
'Golden-haired,' from the Armenian.

Vosgedzin — Ոսկեծին
Vosgedzir — Ոսկեծիր
'Created of gold,' from the Armenian.

Vosgehad — Ոսկեհատ
'Gold nugget,' from the Armenian.

Vosgeher — Ոսկեհեր
Vosgehour — Ոսկեհուր
'Golden-haired,' from the Armenian.

Vosgesar — Ոսկեսար
'Formed of gold,' from the Armenian.

Vosgetel — Ոսկեթել
'Golden thread,' from the Armenian.

Vosgevan — Ոսկեվան
From Vosgevan, a village in Armenia.

Vosgi — Ոսկի
'Gold,' from the Armenian.

Vrejouhi/Vrezhouhi — Վրեժուհի
'Woman of vengeance,' from the Armenian.

Յ

Yar — Եար
'Sweetheart,' from the Armenian.

Yeghisapet — Եղիսաբեթ
'She who has taken God's vow,' from the Hebrew.
The Armenian form of **Elizabeth**.
Alternative forms: **Yeghis** (Եղիս), **Yeghisé** (Եղիսէ),
Yeghsa (Եղսա), **Yeghsig** (Եղսիկ),
and **Yeghso** (Եղսո).

Yeghnar — Եղնար
Yeghner — Եղներ
'Deer,' from the Armenian *yeghn.*
Familiar form: **Yeghnig** (Եղնիկ).

Yepraksé — Եփրաքսէ
'Kind deed,' from the Greek.
Familiar form: **Yebo** (Եպո).

Yeprouhi — Եփրուհի
'Fruitful,' or 'faithful,' from the Hebrew.

Yeranouhi — Երանուհի
'Lucky,' from the Armenian *yerani* 'blessed.'
Alternative forms: **Yeran** (Երան), **Yeraniag** (Երանեակ),
and **Yeranig** (Երանիկ).

Yeraskh — Երասխ
From Araks, the name of the national river of Armenia.

Yeraz — Երազ
'Dream,' from the Armenian.
Familiar form: **Yerazig** (Երազիկ).

Yerchangouhi — Երջանկուհի
'Lucky maiden,' from the Armenian.

Yerchanig — Երջանիկ
'Lucky,' from the Armenian.

Yerevag — Երեվակ
'Saturn,' from the Armenian.

Yester — Եսթեր
'Star,' from the Persian.

58

Yeter — Եթեր
'Ether,' from the Armenian.

Yeva — Եվա
'Life-giving woman,' from the Hebrew. The Armenian form of **Eve**.

Yevkiné — Եվգինէ
'Aristocratic,' from the Greek.

Yevnigé — Եվնիկե
'Successful,' from the Greek *eunike*. The Armenian form of **Eunice**.

Yevpimé — Եվփիմէ
'Lucky,' from the Greek.

Youghaper — Ուղաբեր
'Fragrance bearer,' from the Armenian.
Familiar forms: **Youghig** (Ուղիկ), and **Yougho** (Ուղo).

Z

Zabel — Զապել
'God's vow,' from the Hebrew. The Armenian form of **Isabelle**.
Zabel Asadour (known as Sibyl; 1863-1934), poet, novelist, and defender of women's rights, based in Constantinople.
Zabèle Essayan (1878-1943), French-born writer and thinker.

Zanan — Զանան
Zanazan — Զանազան
'Different,' from the Armenian.
Familiar forms: **Zani** (Զանի), and **Zano** (Զանo).

Zaré — Զարէ
'Gold,' from the Persian.

59

Zarmantoukhd — Զարմանդուխտ
'Cousin,' from the Persian *zar* 'uncle,' and *dokhtar* 'daughter.'
Alternative forms: **Zarman** (Զարման), and **Zarmant** (Զարմանդ).
Familiar forms: **Zarmig** (Զարմիկ), **Zarmo** (Զարմo),
and **Zarmouhi** (Զարմուհի).

Zarminé — Զարմինէ
'Golden,' from the Armenian.

Zarouhi — Զարուհի
'Golden maiden,' from the Persian.
Familiar forms: **Zara** (Զարա), **Zarig** (Զարիկ), and **Zaro** (Զարo).
Queen Zarouhi (second century), wife of King Dikran I of Armenia.

Zartar — Զարդար
'Ornament,' from the Armenian *zart.*
Familiar forms: **Zart** (Զարդ), and **Zarto** (Զարդo).

Zartig — Զարդիկ
Zartouhi — Զարդուհի
'Ornament,' from the Armenian *zart.*

Zepur — Զեփիւռ
'Zephyr,' from the Armenian.
Familiar form: **Zepurig** (Զեփիւռիկ).

Zhpit — ժպիդ
'The one who laughs,' from the Armenian.

Zmroukhd — Զմրուխտ
'Emerald,' from the Armenian.

Zoulal — Զուլալ
'Crystal clear,' from the Armenian.

Zvart — Զուարթ
'Joy,' from the Armenian.

ARMENIAN
BOYS'
NAMES

A

Abah — Ապահ
'Courageous,' from the Armenian.

Abaven — Ապաւէն
'Right-hand man,' from the Armenian.

Acher — Աչեր
'Eyes,' from the Armenian *ach* 'eye.'

Adam — Ադամ
Adom/Adovm — Ատոմ
'Man,' or 'earth,' from the Hebrew.
An Armenian form of **Adam**.
Saint Adovm Knouni (?-451), patriot and martyr.

Adis/Adiss — Ատիս
'Glad tidings,' from the Armenian.
Adiss Harmandian (1945-), Lebanese-born popular singer based in the U.S.

Adroushan — Ատրուշան
'Pagan altar,' from the Armenian.
Familiar form: **Adrouni** (Ատրունի).

Aghajan — Աղաջան
'Dearest lord,' or 'lord of my heart,'
from the Persian *agha* 'lord,' and *jan* 'heart.'

Aghan — Աղան
'Noble,' from the Armenian.

Aghasi — Աղասի
'His lord,' from the Ottoman Turkish.
Aghassi Tour-Sarkissian (1871-1937), Armenian revolutionary,
and one of the leaders of the Zeitoun insurrection of 1895.
Andre Agassi (1970-), U.S. tennis player.

Aghaton — Աղաթոն
'Good,' from the Greek.

Aghavart — Աղավարդ
'Lord of the rose,' from the Persian *agha* 'lord,' and *vard* 'rose.'

Aghazar — Աղազար
'God is my helper,' from the Hebrew.

Agheg — Աղեկ
'Kind-hearted,' from the Armenian.

Agheksandr — Աղեքսանդր
'Protector of men,' from the Greek. The Armenian form of **Alexander**.
Familiar form: **Agheksan** (Աղեքսան).

Aghvor — Աղւոր
'Handsome,' from the Armenian.

Agish — Ակիշ
'Hook,' from the Armenian.

Agnouni — Ակնունի
'Jewel,' from the Armenian.

Agop — Ակոբ
'Follower of God,' from the Hebrew Yaaqob.
An Armenian form of **Jacob** or **James**.
Agop Terzan, French astronomer and theoretician.

Agounik — Ակունիք
From the name of the peak of the Mountains of Vasbouragan.

64

Aharon — Ահարոն
'Mountaineer,' from the Hebrew. The Armenian form of **Aaron**.

Airoug — Այրուկ
'Man,' from the Armenian *ayr*.

Aivaz — Այվազ
'Substitute,' from the Arabic *awaz*.

Alakiaz — Ալագեազ
'Throne of the Spring,' from the Armenian.

Alan/Alain — Ալան
'Harmonious,' from the Celtic.
Alan Hovhaness (Chakmajian; 1911-2000), classical and church composer.
Alain Prost (1955-), French champion Formula One racer.
Alain Boghossian (1970-), French international soccer player and member of
France's 1998 World Cup winning squad.

Aleksander — Ալեքսանդր
'Protector of men,' from the Greek.
The Armenian form of **Alexander**.
Familiar forms: Alek (Ալեք), Aleks (Ալեքս),
Alexan (Ալեքսան), and Axel (Աքսել).
Axel Paghounts (pen-name of Alexander Tevossian; 1899-1937), Armenian writer.
Alex Manoogian (1901-1996), the U.S. auto and construction magnate
who invented the single-handle faucet and founded Masco Corp.
Alek Keshishian (1965-), video and movie director whose films include
Madonna's 'Truth or Dare.'

Alemshah — Ալեմշah
'King of the world,' from the Persian *alem* 'world,' and *shah* 'king.'

Alishan — Ալիշան
'Noble person,' from the Teutonic.

Alpiar — Ալփիար
'Heroic,' from the Armenian.

65

Amadoun — Ամադուն
Amadouni — Ամադունի
From the name of a famous Armenian princely dynasty.

Amanor — Ամանոր
'New Year,' from the Armenian.

Amanos — Ամանոս
From the name of a mountain range in Cilicia.

Amasia — Ամասիա
'Power of God,' the name of a city in Western Armenia.
Familiar form: **Amas** (Ամաս).

Amir — Ամիր
'Prince,' from the Arabic.

Amour — Ամուր
'Steadfast,' from the Armenian.

Amrots — Ամրոց
'Fortress,' from the Armenian.

Anania — Անանիա
'Filled with God's grace,' from the Hebrew and Assyrian.
Familiar form: **Ananig** (Անանիկ).
Anania of Shirag, seventh-century mathematician and astronomer.

Anasdas — Անաս{դ}տաս
'Resurrected,' from the Greek.
Anastas Mikoyan (1895-1978), Communist revolutionary and president of the Soviet Union.

Andon — Անտոն
'Matchless,' from the Latin. The Armenian form of **Anthony**.
Saint Andon (?-330), Armenian monk known for his pious works.
Antonio Kandir (Kandirian; 1953-), Brazilian politician and Minister of State.

Anoushavan — Անուշավան
'Immortal soul,' from the Persian.
Anoushavan der Ghevontian (1887-1961), Armenian composer of classical music.

Antoul — Անդուլ
'Unceasingly,' from the Armenian.

Antranig — Անդրանիկ
'Firstborn,' from the Armenian.
Familiar form: **Anto** (Անդո).
Antranig Ozanian (Shabin-Karahissar; 1865-1927), Armenian revolutionary and military leader.

Antreas — Անդրէաս
'Virile,' from the Greek.

Antsrev — Անձրեւ
'Rain,' from the Armenian.

Apel — Աբէլ
'Sorrow,' from the Hebrew.

Apisoghom — Աբիսողոմ
'Father of peace,' from the Hebrew. The Armenian form of **Absolom**.
Familiar form: **Apig** (Աբիկ).

Apkar — Աբքար
'Head man,' from the Armenian *avak* 'senior,' and *ayr* 'man,'
or the Arabic *abkar* 'great man.'
King Apkar, first-century Armenian king of Edessa, saint and convert.

Apov — Աբով
'Confident one,' from the Armenian.
Apov (17th century), founder of the Melik-Apovian dynasty, rulers of Gulistan.

Apraham — Աբրահամ
'Father of the people,' from the Hebrew
Familiar forms: **Abro** (Աբրո), and **Apo** (Աբո).
Saint Apraham (?-454), deacon and martyr.

67

Ara — Արա
The name of the Ancient Armenian God of Spring.
Familiar form: **Arayig** (Արայիկ).
Prince Ara, the son of the Armenian King Aram, Haig's successor in ancient times.
Ara Parseghian (1923-), U.S. coach of the Notre Dame football team.

Arakadz — Արագած
'Throne of the goddess of Spring,' from the name of
Mount Arakadz in Armenia.

Arakel — Առակել
'Disciple,' from the Armenian.

Aram — Արամ
'Royal highness,' of ancient origin.
Familiar form: **Aramig** (Արամիկ).
King Aram, Haig's successor to the Armenian throne in ancient times.
Aram Khachaturian (1903-1978), Armenian composer of classical music,
renowned especially for his ballet 'Spartacus.'

Aramayis — Արամայիս
'Child of Spring,' from the Armenian.
Familiar forms: **Armavis** (Արմավիս), and **Armayis** (Արմայիս).

Aramazt — Արամազդ
'Supreme wisdom,' from the name of the Ancient Persian God.

Arantsar — Առանձար
An ancient name of unknown origin.

Ararad/Ararat — Արարատ
From Ararat, the name of Armenia's Holy Mountain,
the place where Noah landed the Ark after the Great Flood.

Araz — Արազ
From the name of an Armenian river.
Familiar forms: **Arazi** (Արազի), and **Arazig** (Արազիկ).

Archoug — Արջուկ
'Little bear cub,' from the Armenian *arch* 'bear cub.'

Ardag — Արտակ
'Swift,' from the Pahlavi.

Ardashes — Արտաշէս
'Joyous light,' from the Pahlavi.
Alternative forms: **Ardash** (Արտաշ), **Arden** (Արտէն), and **Ardo** (Արտո).
Familiar form: **Ardoush** (Արտուշ).
Ardashes (Artaxias), founder of the ancient Armenian Ardashessian (Artaxid) dynasty.

Ardashir — Արտաշիր
'Fiery lion,' from the Persian.

Ardavan — Արտավան
'Fiery justice,' from the Persian.

Ardavazt — Արտավազդ
'Lasting justice,' from the Persian.
Ardavazt Pelechian (1938-), Armenian film-maker based in France.

Ardem — Արտէմ
Ardemi — Արտէմի
'Fire of life,' from the Greek. The masculine form of
Artemis, the Greek goddess of the Moon.
Artem Mikoyan (1905-1970), Soviet designer of the MiG fighter aircraft.

Arden — Արտէն
Ardo — Արտո
'Ardent,' from the Latin

Ardouyd — Արտոյտ
'Lark,' from the Armenian.
Familiar form: **Ardoudig** (Արտուտիկ).

Ardzat — Արծաթ
'Silver,' from the Armenian.

69

Ardziv — Արծիւ
'Eagle,' from the Armenian.
Familiar forms: **Ardzvi** (Արծւի), and **Ardzvin** (Արծւին).

Ardzroun — Արծրունն
Ardzrouni — Արծրունի
The name of a famous Armenian royal dynasty.

Ared — Արեդ
An ancient name of unknown origin.

Arek — Արեք
'Sun god,' the name of the ancient Armenian god of the Sun.

Aren — Արեն
From the name of a town and lake in Western Armenia.

Arev — Արեւ
'Sun,' from the Armenian.

Arevhad — Արեւհատ
'Sun seed,' from the Armenian *arev* 'sun,' and *hadig* 'grain.'

Arevshad — Արեվշատ
'Long life,' from the Armenian.

Ari — Արի
'Brave,' from the Hebrew.

Arin — Արին
'Blood,' from the Armenian.

Arisdag — Արիստակ
Arisdages — Արիստակես
'Prince,' from the Greek
Familiar form: **Aris** (Արիս).
Catholicos Aristages (?-333), saint and martyr.
Aristak Hovanessian (1812-1878), composer and musicologist pioneer of
classical Armenian music.

Ariudz — Առիւծ
'Lion,' from the Armenian.

Arka — Արքա
'King,' from the Armenian.

Arkam — Արքամ
'Strength,' from the Ancient Persian.
Arkam, the founder of the Armenian Mouratsan royal dynasty.

Arman — Արման
'Armenian,' from the Armenian.

Armash — Արմաշ
The name of an Armenian town, and a renowned seminary.

Armavir — Արմաւիր
The name of the first capital of Armenia.

Armenag — Արմենակ
From **Armaniag**, the name of the son of the Father of the Armenian people, **Haig**.
Familiar forms: **Armen** (Արմէն), **Armeni** (Արմենի), **Armig** (Արմիկ), **Armis** (Արմիս), **Armo** (Արմo), and **Aro** (Արo).
Armen Dikranian (1879-1950), Armenian classical composer whose works include the famous opera 'Anoush.'

Arnag — Առնակ
'Virile,' from the Armenian.

Arne — Արնէ
Arno — Արնo
'Eagle,' from the Armenian.

Aroushan — Առուշան
'Bright,' from the Persian.

Arpag — Արբակ
An ancient Iranian name of unknown origin.

Arpiar — Արփիար
'Heroic,' from the Armenian.

Arpoun — Արբրունն
'Power,' from the Armenian.

Arsen — Արսէն
'Virile,' from the Greek.

Arshag — Արշակ
'Little bear cub,' from the Armenian *arch* 'bear cub.'

Arshalouys — Արշալույս
'Sunrise,' from the Armenian.

Arsham — Արշամ
'Strong as a bear,' from the Persian.

Arshavir — Արշաւիր
'Virile,' from the Persian.
Familiar forms: **Arshé** (Արշէ), and **Arshen** (Արշէն).
Saint Arshen (?-454), priest and martyr.

Artar — Ardar
'Just,' from the Armenian.

Artin — Արթին
Arto — Արթo
Familiar forms of **Haroutiun** (Յարութիւն).

Artoun — Արդրունն
'Ever vigilant,' from the Armenian.

Artsan — Արձան
'Monument,' from the Armenian.

Arti — Արդի
'Modern,' from the Armenian.

Arzouman — Զրգուման
'Desire,' from the Persian.

Asbed — Ասպետ
'Knight,' from the Armenian.

Asdvadzadour — Աստուածատուր
'Gift of God,' from the Armenian.
Alternative forms: **Asadour** (Ասատուր), and **Dadour** (Տատուր).
Asdvadzadour, the name given to the saint and martyr Makhoj, circa 550.
Oscar Banker (real name Asatour Sarafian; 1920-), U.S. inventor of
the auto transmission and the tetanus inoculation gun.

Ashnag — Աշնակ
The name of a river in Armenia and the summit of Mount Arakadz.

Ashod — Աշոտ
An ancient name of unknown origin.
King Ashod, founder of the Pakradouniats royal dynasty.
Henri Verneuil (real name Ashot Malakian; 1920-), Turkish-born French movie
producer and director.

Askanaz — Ասքանազ
An ancient name for Armenia and the Armenians.

Asoghig — Ասողիկ
'Speaker,' from the Armenian.

Atam/Adam — Ատամ
'Created from the earth,' from the Hebrew.
An Armenian form of **Adam**.

Atig — Աթիկ
'Little horse,' from the Armenian.

Atom — Ատոմ

An alternative form of **Atam** (Ատամ).

Atom Egoyan (1961-), award-winning Canadian film-maker and screenwriter.

Avak — Աւաք

'Great,' from the Armenian.

Avedig — Աւետիկ
Avedis — Աւետիս

'Glad tidings,' from the Armenian.

Alternative form: Aved (Աւետ).

Familiar forms: **Avig** (Աւիկ), **Avis** (Աւիս), and **Avo** (Աւօ).

Avo Uvezian (1926-), Lebanese-born Dominican maker of cigars.
Avedig Evdokiatsi (1657-1711), Armenian patriarch of Constantinople and Jerusalem incarcerated by the French in the Bastille.
Avedis Aharonian (1866-1948), politician and writer who, in 1920, signed the Treaty of Sèvres as President of the Delegation of the Republic of Armenia.

Azad — Ազատ

'Free,' from the Persian.

Azad Manoukian (1878-1958), educationalist and children's book writer who worked extensively in Armenia and Georgia.

Azarig — Ազարիկ

'With God's help,' from the Hebrew.

Azkaser — Ազգասէր

'Great patriot,' from the Armenian.

Aznvagan — Ազնուական

'Noble,' from the Armenian.

Aznavor — Ազնաւոր
Aznavour — Ազնաւուր

'Noble one,' from the Armenian.

Charles (Shahnour) Aznavour (1924-), French international singer, songwriter, and actor.

B

Bab — Պապ
'Father of all fathers,' from the Persian.
Alternative form: Babin (Պապին).
Familiar forms: Babig (Պապիկ),
and Baboug (Պապուկ).

Badrig — Պատրիկ
'Royalty,' from the Greek. The Armenian form of **Patrick**.

Badvagan — Պատուական
'Man of honor,' from the Armenian.

Baghdasar — Պաղտասար
'May the Lord protect the king,' from the Assyrian.
Familiar forms: Baghdig (Պաղտիկ),
and Baghdo (Պաղտo).
Ross Baghdasarian, U.S. cartoonist and creator of 'The Chipmunks.'

Baikar — Պայքար
'Noble struggle,' from the Armenian.

Bajouyj — Պանուն
'Priceless one,' from the Armenian.

Bantoukhd — Պանդուխտ
'Wanderer,' from the Armenian.

Bared — Պարետ
'Guardian,' from the Armenian.

Barkev — Պարգև
'Gift,' from the Armenian.

Barouyr — Պարուր
'Completeness,' from the Armenian.

Parouyr Sevak (1924-1971), celebrated Armenian poet and writer.

Barsam — Պարսամ
'Son of the abstainer,' from the Assyrian.

Bartev — Պարթեւ
'Giant,' from the name of the ancient Parthian tribe.

Barzik — Պարզիկ
'Sincere one,' from the Armenian.

Bedros — Պետրոս
'Rock,' from the Greek *petros*. An Armenian form of **Peter**.
Familiar forms: **Bebo** (Պեպո), **Bedig** (Պետիկ), and **Bedo** (Պետո).

Benon — Պենոն
An ancient name of unknown origin.

Benon Sevon (1937-), born in Cyprus, the highest ranking Armenian in the United Nations.

Berj — Պերճ
'Best of all,' from the Armenian.

Boghos — Պողոս
'Little one,' from the Latin *paulus*. The Armenian form of **Paul**.
Eric Bogosian (1953-), U.S. satirical writer and actor.
Boghos Noubar Pasha (1851-1930), diplomat and Minister of Foreign Affairs in Egypt.

Bourag — Պուրակ
'Forest,' from the Armenian.

Bsag — Պսակ
'Crown,' from the Armenian.

Bsdig — Պստիկ
'Young one,' from the Armenian.

C

Chan — Չան
'Beloved soul,' from the Persian *jan*.

Chani — Չանի
'Beloved one,' from the Persian.

Chanipeg — Չանիբեկ
'Lord beloved soul,' from the Persian.
Familiar form: **Chanig** (Չանիկ).

Charents — Չարենծ
'Mischievous,' from the Armenian.

Chivan — Չիւան
Chivani — Չիւանի
'Young man,' from the Persian *jivan*.
Chivani (1846-1909), renowned bard ('ashoug' or 'kousan') and songwriter who traveled and worked throughout the Caucasus – the second greatest ashoug after Sayat Nova.

Christapor — Քրիստափոր
'Christ-bearer,' from the Greek. The Armenian form of **Christopher**.
Familiar form: **Chris** (Քրիս).

D

Dadour — Տատուր
A short form of **Asdvadzadour** (Աստուածատուր)
or **Diradour** (Տիրատուր).

77

Dajad — Դաճատ
'Gift,' from the Ancient Persian.
Familiar form: **Dalo** (Դալօ).

Daniel — Դանիէլ
'God is my judge,' from the Hebrew.
Bishop Daniel (?-348), saint, missionary, and martyr.
Daniel Varuzhan (real name Daniel Chibukkyarian; 1884-1915),
Armenian poet and writer.

Daron — Տարոն
'He who possesses good,' from the Persian, or from the name of the
province of Western Armenia, with its center at Moush, now in Turkey.

Datev — Տաթեւ
From the name of a monastery in Armenia.

David — Դաւիթ
'Beloved one,' from the Hebrew.
David Shakarian, U.S. businessman and founder
of the General Nutrition Center.
David G. Hessayon (1928-), Cyprus-born British creator and publisher
of the bestselling 'Expert Gardener' series.

Davros — Տաւրոս
From the name of the Taurus Mountains.

Deroun — Տէրուն
Derouni — Տէրունի
'Special to God,' from the Armenian.

Dikran — Տիգրան
'Bowman,' from the Old Persian.
Familiar forms: **Dik** (Տիգ), and **Diko** (Տիգօ).
King Dikran II the Great (121-54), famous for conquering Syria,
Mesopotamia, and part of Asia Minor.

Dikris — Տիգրիս
From the name of the River Tigris.

Dir — Տիր
The Armenian god of the Arts.

Diradour — Տիրատուր
'God-given,' from the Armenian.

Dirair — Տիրայր
'Man of God,' from the Armenian.

Diran — Տիրան
'Father of all Gods,' from the Persian.

Dirazt — Տիրազդ
'Inspired by God,' from the Armenian.

Diro — Տիրո
'Gift of God,' from **Diradour** (Տիրատուր).

Diroug — Տիրու
'Prince,' from the Armenian.

Donabed — Տօնապետ
'Chieftain of the festival,' from the Armenian.

Donag — Տօնակ
Donagan — Տօնական
Donig — Տօնիկ
'Festival,' from the Armenian.

Drtad — Տրդատ
'Gift of God,' from the Armenian.
Familiar form: **Dirit** (Տիրիտ).
*King Drtad (?-330), Armenian saint and martyr, the first monarch to convert
to Christianity.*

Dzar — Ծառ
Dzaroug — Ծառուկ
'Tree,' from the Armenian *dzar*.
Familiar form: **Dzarig** (Ծառիկ).

79

Dzeron — Ծերոն
Dzeroun — Ծերուն
'Old man,' from the Armenian.

Dzovag — Ծովակ
'Blue-eyes,' from the Armenian.

Ե

Edward — Եդուարդ
'Guardian of the treasury,' from the Anglo-Saxon *ead* 'treasure,'
and *ward* 'keeper.'
Eduardo Eurnekian (1933-), Argentinian media and tourism businessman.

Emile — Եմիլ
'Eager,' from the Latin.
Emile Lahoud (1936-), general and president of Lebanon.

Emin — Էմին
'Trustworthy,' from the Arabic *amin* 'safe.'

Emmanuel — Էմմանուէլ
'God is with us,' from the Hebrew *Immanuel.*

Ֆ

Firouz — Ֆիրուզ
'Conqueror,' from the Persian.

Frig — Ֆրիկ
'Peaceful ruler,' from the Old Germanic *frid* 'peace,'
and *rik* 'rich man.' The Armenian form of **Frederick**.

Գ

Gaboudag — Կապուտակ
Gabouyd — Կապւյտ
'Blue one,' from the Armenian *gabouyd* 'blue.'
Familiar form: **Gaboudig** (Կապուտիկ).

Gabriel — Կապրիէլ
'God is powerful,' from the Hebrew *gabar* 'to have strength,'
and *El* 'God.'

Gagig — Գագիկ
An ancient name of Assyrian origin.
*Gagig, the name shared by several princes and kings from the Pakradouni dynasty
and the founders of Ani.*

Gagos — Կակոս
'Belonging to the Lord,' from the Greek.

Gaidar — Կայտառ
'Full of life,' from the Latin *gaius* 'lively.'

Gaidzag — Կայծակ
'Lightning,' from the Armenian.

Gamsar — Կամսար
'Majesty,' from the Persian.

Ganach — Կանաչ
'Green one,' from the Armenian.

Gantegh — Կանթեղ
'Lantern,' from the Armenian.

Garabed — Կարապետ
'Guide,' from the Armenian.
Alternative forms: Garb (Կարպ), Garbis (Կարպիս),
Garig (Կարիկ), and Garo (Կարո).
Familiar form: Garoush (Կարուշ).

Gary Kasparov (1963-), *Azerbaijan-born Armenian chess master and world champion,
and Representative in the Russian Parliament.*

Garen — Կարեն
An ancient name of Iranian origin.

Garin — Քարին
From the ancient name of Erzroum, a city in Western Armenia.

Garod — Կարոտ
'Longing,' from the Armenian.

Gdrij — Կրտրիճ
'Heroic.'

Gharib — Ղարիպ
'Stranger,' or 'foreigner,' from the Arabic *gharib*.

Ghazar — Ղազար
Ghazaros — Ղազարոս
'Helped by God,' from the Hebrew *Eleazar*.

The Armenian form of **Lazarus**.
Alternative forms: **Ghazig** (Ղազիկ), **Ghazo** (Ղազո), and **Lazar** (Լազար).

Ghevont — Ղեւոնդ
'Lion,' from the Greek.
Father Ghevont Alishan (real name Kerovpe Alishanian; 1820-1901), historian, poet, geographer, translator, born in Constantinople and one of the Mekhitarist Fathers in Venice.

Ghougas — Ղուկաս
'Resurrection,' from the Armenian.

Giligia — Կիլիկիա
From the name of the kingdom of Cilicia, in Asia Minor.

Giragos — Կիրակոս
'Belonging to the Lord,' from the Armenian.
Giragos Gandzagetsi (1200-1271), theologian and historian who was the Armenian Ambassador to the Court of the Great Mongol.

Giuregh — Կիւրեղ
'Loved by the Lord,' from the Greek.

Gomidas — Կոմիտաս
'Long flowing hair,' from the Greek.
Gomidas (Komitas) Vartabed (real name Soghomon Soghomonian; 1869-1935), pioneering musicologist of Armenian church and folk music.

Goms — Կոմս
'Prince,' from the Armenian form of the French 'comte.'

Goriun — Կորիւն
'Lionheart,' from the Armenian.

Gosdantin — Կոստանդին
'Constant,' from the Latin.
Familiar form: **Gosdan** (Կոստան).
Gosdan Zarian (1885-1969), Armenian philosopher and historical novel writer.

Guregh — Կիւրեղ
'Loved by the Lord,' from the Greek.

H

Hagop — Յակոբ
'Follower of God,' from the Hebrew *Yaaqob*.
The Armenian form of **Jacob** and **James**.
Alternative forms: **Ago** (Ակօ), **Agop** (Ակոբ),
Agou (Ակու), **Agoup** (Ակուբ), and **Ago** (Ակօ).
Familiar forms: **Hago** (Յակօ), **Hagopig** (Յակոբիկ),
Hagopos (Յակոբոս), and **Hagovp** (Յակովբ).

Hagop Hagopian (1923-), international painter of Egyptian-Cypriot origin.
James Bagian (1952-), American astronaut.

Hagopchan — Յակոբջան
'Cherished follower of God,' from the Hebrew *Yaaqob*
and the Persian *jan* 'dear.'

Hagopshah — Յակոբշահ
'Lord follower of God,' from the Hebrew *Yaaqob*
and the Persian *shah* 'king.'

Haipert — Հայբերդ
'Armenian fortress,' from the Armenian.

Haig — Հայկ
'Giant' – descendant of Noah and first king of the Armenians.
From his name are derived *Hay* 'Armenian,' and *Hayastan* 'Armenia.'
Alternative form: **Haigag** (Հայկակ).
Familiar form: **Haigo** (Հայկօ).

Haigaram — Հայկարամ
The combination of **Haig** (Հահկ) and **Aram** (Արամ).

Haigasar — Հայկասար
'Haig's mountain,' from the Armenian.

Haigaser — Հայկասեր
Haigaz — Հայկազ
Haigazoun — Հայկազուն
'Descended from Haig,' from the Armenian.

Haigashen — Հայկաշէն
'Created by Haig,' from the Armenian.

Haigazad — Հայկազատ
The combination of **Haig** (Հաիկ) and **Azad** (Ազատ).
Alternative form: **Haigazoun** (Հաիկազունունն).

Hairabed — Հայրապետ
'Patriarch,' from the Armenian.
Familiar form: **Hairo** (Հայրո).

Hairazad — Հայրազատ
'Faithful,' from the Armenian.

Hairenik — Հայրենիք
'Homeland,' from the Armenian.

Hairi — Հայրի
'Father,' from the Armenian *hayr* 'father.'
Familiar form: **Hairig** (Հայրիկ)

Haitoug — Հայդուկ
'Warrior,' from the Armenian.

Haivart — Հայվարդ
'Armenian rose,' from the Armenian *hay* 'Armenian,' and *vart* 'rose.'

Hamaz — Համազ
Hamazasb — Համազասպ
'Possessor of many horses,' from the Persian.
Familiar forms: **Hamag** (Համակ), **Hamig** (Համիկ), and **Hamo** (Համո).
Saint Hamazasb Ardzrounig (?-786), aristocrat, revolutionary, and martyr.

85

Hamel — Համէլ
Hamlig — Համլիկ
An ancient name of unknown origin.

Hampartsoum — Համբարձում
'Ascension,' from the Armenian.
Alternative forms: **Hampar** (Համբար), **Hamparts** (Համբարձ), **Hampig** (Համբիկ), and **Hampo** (Համբո).
Hambartsum Limonjian (1768-1839), musicologist who reformed Armenian classical and church music.

Hapet — Յապէթ
'Handsome one,' from the Armenian.
Alternative form: **Apetig** (Աբեթիկ).

Harazad — Հարազատ
'Genuine,' from the Armenian.

Harma — Հարմա
Harmig — Հարմիկ
An ancient name of unknown origin.

Haroutiun — Յարութիւն
'Resurrection,' from the Armenian.
Alternative forms: **Haro** (Յարո), and **Harout** (Յարութ).
Familiar form: **Artin** (Արթին).
Haroutiun Zildjian, 17th-century maker of bells based in Constantinople.
Haroutioun Sayatian (known as Sayat Nova; 1712-1795), renowned bard ('ashoug' or 'kousan') and songwriter who worked throughout the Caucasus.

Hayasdan — Հայաստան
'Land of Armenia,' from the Armenian.

Hayaser — Հայասեր
'Children of Haig,' from the Armenian.

Hayashen — Հայաշէն
'Created by the Armenians,' from the Armenian.

Hayots — Հայոծ
'Armenian nation,' from the Armenian.

Hazarabed — Հազարապետ
'Leader in battle,' from the Armenian.
Alternative form: **Hazar** (Հազար).

Heros — Հերոս
'Hero,' from the Armenian.

Hetoum — Հեթում
'Wise judge,' from the Arabic.

Hmayag — Հմայեակ
'Talisman,' from the Armenian.

Hoki — Հոգի
'Spirit,' from the Armenian.

Horizon — Հորիզոն
'Horizon,' from the Armenian.

Hounan — Յունան
Houno — Յունօ
'Dove,' from the Hebrew.

Houys — Յոյս
'Hope,' from the Armenian.
Familiar form: **Housig** (Յուսիկ).
Catholicos Housig (?-347), saint and martyr.

Hovagim — Յովակիմ
'With God's strength,' from the Hebrew *Yohaqim*.
Familiar form: **Hovag** (Յովակ).

Hovasap — Յովասափ
'God the judge,' from the Hebrew.

87

Hovel — Յովէլ
'Pleasing to God,' from the Hebrew.

Hovhan — Յովհան
An alternative form of **Hovhannes** (Յովհաննէս).
*Catholicos Hovhan Otsnetsi (?-728), saint, philosopher, and one of
the Armenian Church Fathers.*

Hovhannes — Յովհաննէս
'Gift of God,' from the Hebrew *Yohaman.*
Alternative forms: **Hovan/Hovann** (Յովան), **Ohan** (Ոհան),
and **Ohannes** (Ոհաննէս).
Familiar form: **Hovhanig** (Յովհանիկ) and **Hovig** (Յովիկ).
Saint Hovhannes (?-604), one of the hermit martyrs called the Seven Witnesses.
*Saint Hovhannes Vorodnetsi (1315-1388), theologian, and defender of
the Armenian Church.*
Hovhaness Aivazovsky (1817-1900), Russian-born Armenian painter of seascapes.

Hovig — Հովիկ
'Breeze,' from the Armenian.

Hovnan — Յovնան
'Dove,' from the Hebrew.

Hovsep — Յովսէփ
'May God send more children,' from the Hebrew *Yosefyah.*
An Armenian form of **Joseph.**
Catholicos Hovsep (?-454), saint and martyr.

Hrad — Հրատ
'Mars,' from the Armenian.

Hrag — Հրակ
'Eyes of fire,' from the Armenian.

Hrahad — Հրահատ
'Spark of fire,' from the Armenian.

Hrair — Հրայր
'Man of fire,' from the Armenian.

Hrant — Հրանդ
'Flame,' from the Armenian.

Hratch — Հրաչ
'Fiery eyes,' from the Armenian.
Familiar forms: **Hratchia** (Հրաչիա), and **Hratchig** (Հրաչիկ).
Hratchia Ajarian (1876-1953), famous linguist, scholar and writer of a monumental five-volume dictionary of Armenian first names.

Hrayr — Հրայր
'Man of fire,' from the Armenian.

Hraztan — Հրազդան
The name of the river that flows from Lake Sevan in Armenia.

I

Isahag — Իսահակ
'The one who makes God smile,' from the Hebrew *Yitzhaq*.
The Armenian form of **Isaac**.

Ishkhan — Իշխան
'Prince,' from the Armenian.

J

Jani — Ճանի
Jano — Ճանo
'Beloved soul,' from the Persian.
Familiar form: **Janig** (Ճանիկ).

Jarbig — Ճարպիկ
'Quick of wit,' from the Armenian.

Jermag — Ճերմակ
'Fair,' from the Armenian.

Jirair — Ժիրայր
'Agile,' from the Armenian.
Familiar forms: **Jirig** (Ժիրիկ), and **Jiro** (Ժիրo).

Jivan — Ճիվան
'Gift of God,' from the Hebrew *Yohaman*.
The Armenian for **Giovanni**.

Joudig — Ճուտիկ
'Little bird,' from the Armenian *joud* 'chick.'

K

Kachair/Kachayr — Քաջայր
Kachazoun — Քաջազուն
'Valiant,' from the Armenian *kach* 'brave.'
Alternative form: **Kachaz** (Քաջազ).

90

Kacher — Քաշեր
'Valiant ones,' from the Armenian *kach* 'brave.'
Familiar form: **Kachig** (Քաշիկ).

Kail — Գայլ
'Wolf,' from the Armenian.

Kakig — Գագիկ
An ancient name of Assyrian origin.

Kalousd — Գալուստ
'Pentecost,' from the Armenian.
Familiar forms: **Kalig** (Գալիկ), and **Kalo** (Գալո).
*Calouste Gulbenkian (1869-1955), Turkey-born British industrialist and philanthropist
who was one of the creators of the modern oil industry.*

Kants — Գանձ
'Treasure,' from the Armenian.

Kapriel — Գաբրիէլ
'God is powerful,' from the Hebrew root *gabar* 'to have strength,'
and *El* 'God.' The Armenian form of **Gabriel**.
Familiar forms: **Kapig** (Գաբիկ), and **Kapo** (Գապո).

Karekin — Գարեգին
An ancient name of unknown origin.
Familiar forms: **Karen** (Գարէն), **Karig** (Գարիկ), and **Karo** (Գարո).

Karnig — Գառնիկ
'Little lamb,' from the Armenian *karn* 'lamb.'
*Carzou (real name Karnig Zulumian; 1907-),
French-born designer and painter famous for his scenes of Venice.*

Kasbar — Գասպար
'Lord of the treasury.' The Armenian form of **Caspar**.
*Kaspar Ipekian (1883-1952), writer, poet, and politician who founded the Armenian
international cultural association Hamaskain.*

Keghair — Գեղայր
Kegham — Գեղամ
'Handsome man,' from the Armenian.

Keghart — Գեղարդ
From the name of a famous Armenian monastery.

Keghon — Գեղոն
'Glory,' from the Armenian.

Keri — Քերի
'Uncle,' from the Armenian.

Kerovpé — Քերովբէ
'Angel,' from the Armenian.
Familiar forms: **Kero** (Քերո), and **Kerop** (Քերոբ).

Kersam — Գերսամ
'Emigrant,' from the Armenian.

Kevon — Գեւոն
'Glory,' from the Armenian.
Familiar forms: **Kevig** (Գեւիկ), and **Kevo** (Գեւո).

Kevork — Գէորգ
'Farmer,' from the Greek *giorgos*. The Armenian form of **George**.
Kevork Hovnanian, Baghdad-born U.S. home builder
and real estate developer.
George Deukmejian (1928-), U.S. politician and governor of California.
George Gurdjieff (1877-1949), international mystic and spiritual writer.

Khachadour — Խաչատուր
'Follower of Christ.' The Armenian form of **Christian**.
Familiar forms: **Khachi** (Խաչի), **Khacho** (Խաչո), **Khachod**
(Խաչոտ), **Khachoud** (Խաչուտ), **Khachoum** (Խաչում),
Khachoug (Խաչուկ), and **Khechi** (Խեչի).
Khatchadour Apovian (1809-1848), writer and 'father' of the modern Armenian novel.

92

Khachbab — Խաչպապ
'Godfather,' from the Armenian *khach* 'cross,' and *bab* 'father.'

Khacher — Խաչեր
Khacheres — Խաչերես
'Face of the cross,' from the Armenian.

Khachig — Խաչիկ
'Little cross,' from the Armenian.

Khachkar — Խաչքար
'Memorial cross,' from the Armenian.

Khajag — Խաժակ
'Eyes of turquoise,' from the Armenian.

Khat — Խադ
'Sabre,' from the Armenian.

Khigar — Խիկար
'Wise one,' from the Armenian.

Khint — Խինդ
'Happiness,' from the Armenian.

Khntoun — Խնդուն
'Happy,' from the Armenian.

Khoren — Խորէն
'Small sun,' from the Persian.
Saint Khoren (?-454), priest and martyr.
Koren der Harootian, award-winning U.S. sculptor.

Khosdig — Խոստիկ
'Little vow,' from the Armenian *khosdoum* 'vow.'

Khosrov — Խոսրով
'Famous one,' from the Pahlavi.
Familiar form: Khosrig (Խոսրիկ).

Kirk — Քիրք
'Church,' from the Old Norse *kirkja*.
Kirk Kerkorian (1917-), U.S. entrepreneur and property magnate.

Kiud — Գիտտ
'Revelation,' from the Armenian.

Klag — Գլակ
An ancient name of unknown origin.

Knel — Գնէլ
'Gift,' from the Armenian.

Knouni — Գնունի
The name of a famous Armenian princely dynasty.

Kor — Գոռ
'Proud,' from the Armenian.

Kotchar — Քոչար
'Emigrant,' from the Armenian.

Kouj/Kouzh — Գուժ
'Sad tidings,' from the Armenian.

Kourken — Գուրգէն
'Wolf,' from the Persian.
Gourgen Melikian, award-winning writer and academic.
Kourken Alemshah (1907-1947), musician, composer and conductor,
born in Turkey and based in the U.S.

Kousan — Գուսան
'Wandering minstrel,' from the Armenian.

Koushag — Գուշակ
'Soothsayer,' from the Armenian.

Krikor — Գրիգոր
Krikoris — Գրիգորիս
'Watchful,' from the Greek *Gregorios*. The Armenian form of **Gregory**.
Alternative forms: **Koko** (Գոգո), and **Kokor** (Գոգոր).
Familiar form: **Krish** (Գրիշ).

*Saint Krikor Lousavorich (256-326), Father, and Patron Saint of the
Armenian Church, called 'Gregory the Illuminator.'*
Saint Krikor Naregatsi Vartabed (950-1010), author of the 'Nareg,' or
'Book of Lamentations,' and greatest of the Armenian nation's poets and mystics.
Saint Krikor Datevatsi (1346-1410), preacher, and philosopher
often called 'the Second Gregory the Illuminator.'
Krikor Zohrab (1861-1915), writer and politician in Ottoman Turkey.
*Michael Connors (real name Kreker Ohanian; 1925-), U.S. film and
television actor, and star of 'Mannix.'*

L

Lalazar — Լալազար
'Garden of tulips,' from the Persian.

Lavo — Լավո
'Gifted one,' from the Armenian.

Lazar — Լազար
'Helped by God,' from the Hebrew *Eleazar*.
The Armenian form of **Lazarus**.

Leo — Լեո
'Lion,' from the Latin.

Lernig — Լեռնիկ
'Little mountain,' from the Armenian *ler* 'mountain.'

Levon — Լեւոն
'Lion,' from the Greek.
Familiar form: **Levig** (Լեւիկ).

Lorents — Լորենծ
'Crowned with laurels,' from the Latin.
Familiar form: **Lorig** (Լորիկ).

Loris — Լորիս
From Lori, a region in Armenia.

Louseres — Լուսերես
'Shining,' from the Latin.

Loutfi — Լութֆի
'Gracious,' from the Arabic.

Loutfig — Լութֆիկ
'Battle glory,' from the German *Ludwig*.

Louys — Լոյս
Louyser — Լոյսեր
Louyseres — Լոյսերես
'Light.' The Armenian for **Louis**.
Louis Hagopian, advertising and marketing innovator, and writer of slogans like 'Diamonds are forever.'

Madat — Մատաթ
Madatia — Մատաթիա
'Gift of God,' from the Hebrew.

Mado — Մատո
'Martyr,' from the Latin.

Madteos — Մատթէոս
'Gift of God,' from the Hebrew *matht* 'gift,' and *yah* (an abbreviation
for Yahweh 'God'). The Armenian form of **Matthew**.
Alternative forms: Madte (Մատթէ), Madtos (Մատթոս),
Mateos (Մաթէոս), Matevos (Մաթեւոս), Matios (Մաթիոս),
and Matos (Մաթոս).

Magar — Մակար
'Lucky,' from the Greek *makarios*.
*Magar Yegmalian (1856-1905), prolific composer of hymns, and popular
and patriotic songs.*

Maghakia — Մաղաքիա
'Angel,' from the Hebrew

Majag — Մաժակ
An ancient name of unknown origin.

Maksoud — Մաքսուտ
'Guided,' from the Arabic *maqsud* 'purpose.'

Malkhas — Մալխաս
'Favorite,' from the Persian.

Mamigon — Մամիկոն
From the name of the Mamigonians, a famous Armenian princely dynasty.

Mampré — Մամբրէ
'Fertile,' from the Hebrew.

Manan — Մանան
An ancient name of unknown origin.

Manas — Մանաս
Manasé — Մանասէ
'Forgetful,' from the Hebrew.

Mangasar — Մանկասար
'Teacher,' or 'wise one,' from the Armenian.

Manoog/Manoug — Մանուկ
'Child,' from the Armenian.
Familiar form: **Mangig** (Մանկիկ).
Manoug Apeghian (1865-1944), Armenian linguist and scholar.
Richard Manoogian, U.S. industrialist and art collector with a large interest in Masco Corporation.

Manuel — Մանուէլ
'God is with us,' from the Hebrew.
An alternative form of **Emmanuel** (Էմմանուէլ).
Alternative form: **Mano** (Մանo).
Saint Manuel (?-454), priest and martyr.

Mardig — Մարտիկ
'Warrior,' from the Armenian.

Mardin — Մարտին
'Mars,' from the name of the Latin god of war.
The Armenian form of **Martin**.

Mardiros — Մարտիրոս
'Martyr,' from the Latin.
Alternative forms: **Mardo** (Մարտo), **Mrdo** (Մրտo)
and **Mardi** (Մարտի).
Mardiros Sarian (1880-1972), Armenian painter.

Mardouni — Մարտունի
From the name of a city and region in Armenia.

Margos — Մարկոս
'Warrior,' from the Latin. The Armenian form of **Mark**.

Marinos — Մարինոս
'From the sea,' from the Latin.

Mark — Մարգ
'Green meadow,' from the Armenian.

Markar — Մարգար
'Soothsayer,' from the Armenian.

Marmant — Մարմանդ
'Green fields,' from the Armenian.

Marout — Մարութ
Marouta — Մարութա
'Lord of the world,' from the Assyrian.

Martag — Մարդակ
'Source of help,' from the Armenian.

Marzbed — Մարզպետ
'Governor,' from the Pahlavi.

Mashdots — Մաշտոց
'Bearing a tonsure,' from the Armenian.
*Saint Mesrob Mashdots (?-438), translator, writer,
and inventor of the Armenian alphabet.*

Masho — Մաշո
Derived from the Russian.

Masis — Մասիս
A name for the holy mountain of Armenia, Mount Ararat.

Masour — Մասուր
'Dogrose berry,' from the Armenian.

Matsag — Մացակ
An alternative form of **Mnatsagan** (Մնացական).

Matteos — Մատթէոս
An alternative form of **Madteos** (Մատթէոս).

Mayil — Մայիլ
'Lover,' from the Arabic.

Mayis — Մայիս
'May,' from the Armenian.

Mayranoush — Մայրանոյշ
'Mother's favorite,' from the Armenian.

Mazhag — Մաժակ
An ancient name of unknown Eastern origin.

Medzadour — Մեծատուր
'Generous one,' from the Armenian.

Medzig — Մեծիկ
'Little great one,' from *metz* 'great.'

Meghrig — Մեղրիկ
'Little honey,' from *meghr* 'honey.'

Mekhag — Մեխակ
'Carnation,' from the Armenian.

Melik — Մելիք
'King,' from the Arabic *malik*, and a title of Armenian princes.

Melkon — Մելքոն
Melkoum — Մելքում
'King of light,' from the Hebrew.

Meroujan — Մերուժան
'Power of the sun,' from the Pahlavi.
Alternative form: **Merouj** (Մերուժ).

Mesia — Մեսիա
'Messiah,' from the Hebrew.

Mesrob — Մեսրոպ
An ancient name of unknown origin.
Familiar form: **Mesrig** (Մեսիկ).
Saint Mesrob Mashdots *(?-438), translator, writer,
and inventor of the Armenian alphabet.*

Mgrditch — Մկրդիչ
'Baptist,' from the Armenian.
Alternative forms: **Mgo** (Մկո), **Mgoutch** (Մկուչ),
and **Migitch** (Միկիչ).

Mgrdoum — Մկրտում
'Baptism,' from the Armenian.

Mher — Մհեր
Mihr — Միհր
'Friendship,' from the name of the Ancient Persian
god of the Sun.
Mher, a mighty hero from the Armenian legends of old.

Mihran — Միհրան
'Treasure of the sun,' from the Ancient Persian.

Mihrtad — Միհրդատ
'Created by the sun,' from the Ancient Persian.

Mikael/Mikayel — Միքայէլ
'Like unto the Lord,' from the Hebrew.

Minas — Մինաս
'Formidable,' from the Ancient Egyptian.

Mirak — Միրաք
'Little prince,' from the Persian.

Mirijan — Միրիջան
Mirjan — Միրջան
'Lord of the soul,' from the Persian *mir* 'lord,' and *jan* 'soul.'
Familiar forms: **Mirig** (Միրիկ), and **Miro** (Միրո).

Misak — Միսաք
An ancient Hebrew name of unknown origin.

Misha — Միշա
From the Russian familiar form of **Mikhail/Michael**.

Miuron — Միւռոն
'Holy oil,' from the Greek.

Mkhitar — Մխիթար
'Consolation,' from the Armenian.
Familiar form: **Mkho** (Մխո).
Mkhitar (Mekhitar) Sepasdatsi (1676-1749), *founder of the Mekhitarist Armenian Catholic Order in Venice and Vienna, instrumental in the Armenian Renaissance.*

Mleh — Մլեհ
'Handsome,' from the Arabic *malih*.

Mnatsagan — Մնացական
'Long may he live!,' from the Armenian *mnal* 'to live.'
Alternative forms: **Matsag** (Մացակ), **Matso** (Մացo), **Mnats** (Մնաց), **Mno** (Մնo), and **Tsagan** (Ցական).

Momig — Մոմիկ
'Little lantern,' from the Armenian *mom* 'lantern.'

Mourad — Մուրատ
Mouraz — Մուրազ
'Desired,' from the Arabic *murad*.

Mourig — Մուրիկ
'Little beggar,' from the Armenian *mouratsgan*.

Moush — Մուշ
From the name of a city in Western Armenia.
Familiar form: **Moushig** (Մուշիկ).

Moushegh — Մուշեղ
An ancient name of Hattian origin.
Familiar forms: **Mishig** (Միշիկ), and **Mousho** (Մուշո).

Movses — Մովսէս
'Saved from the water,' from the Hebrew,
or 'youth,' from the Ancient Egyptian.
The Armenian form of **Moses**.
Familiar forms: **Mosi** (Մոսի), and **Mosig** (Մոսիկ).
Saint Movses Khorenatsi, *fifth-century martyr and philosopher,
one of the Holy Translators and the father of Armenian history.*

Mshag — Մշակ
'Worker of the earth,' from the Armenian.

Ն

Naghash — Նաղաշ
'Artist,' from the Arabic *naqqash* 'artisan.'

Nahabed — Նահապետ
'Forebear,' from the Armenian.
Nahabed Kouchag, 16th-century Armenian poet and bard.

Nar — Նար
'Flame,' from the Arabic *nar* 'fire.'

Narbey — Նարպեյ
'Fire-lord,' from the Arabic *nar* 'fire,' and Persian *beg* 'lord.'

Nareg — Նարեկ
From the name of a village and its famous Armenian monastery.

Nartos — Նարդոս
'Spikenard,' a flower used for aromatic oils, from the Armenian.

Navasart — Նաւասարդ
The name of the first month in the ancient Armenian calendar.
Alternative form: **Navo** (Նաւո).

Nayiri — Նայիրի
'River,' from one of the ancient names of Armenia.

Nazar — Նազար
'Vision,' from the Arabic *nazar.*

Nazaret — Նազարեթ
The name of the birthplace of Jesus Christ, Nazareth.
Alternative form: **Nazo** (Նազո).

Nazarpeg — Նազարբեկ
'Prince of sight,' from the Arabic *nazar* 'vision,'
and the Persian *beg* 'prince.'

Ned — Նետ
'Arrow,' from the Armenian.

Nerseh — Ներսեհ
Nerses — Ներսէս
'Message,' from the Pahlavi *nerseh* 'word.'
Familiar forms: **Nersig** (Ներսիկ), **Nerso** (Ներսո), and **Neso** (Նեսո).
Saint Nerses the Great (?-373), saint, theologian, and leader of the Armenian Church,
also called 'The Builder.'
Saint Nerses Shnorhali (1102-1173), musician, poet, and writer, also called 'The Graceful.'

Nigoghayos — Նիկողայոս
Nigoghos — Նիկողոս
'Victory of the people,' from the Greek *nike* 'victory,' and *laos* 'people.'
The Armenian form of **Nicholas**.
Alternative form: **Nigol** (Նիգոլ).

Njteh — Նժդեհ
'Foreigner,' or 'stranger,' from the Armenian.
Familiar form: **Njtig** (Նժդիկ).

Norabed — Նորապետ
'New chieftain,' from the Armenian.

Norair/Norayr — Նորայր
'New man,' from the Armenian.

Norhad — Նորհատ
'New one,' from the Armenian.
Familiar form: **Norig** (Նորիկ).

Norvart — Նորվարդ
'New rose,' from the Armenian *nor* 'new,' and *vart* 'rose.'

Noubar — Նուպար
'First fruit,' from the Persian.
*Noubar Pasha (1825-1899), prime minister of Egypt, whose son Boghos Noubar Pasha
(1851-1930) was an international diplomat who founded the Armenian General
Benevolent Union in 1906.*

Noy — Նոյ
'Calm,' from the Hebrew.

Nshan — Նշան
'Omen,' from the Armenian.

Nver — Նուէր
'Gift,' from the Armenian.

Nzhteh — Նժդեհ
'Foreigner,' or 'stranger,' from the Armenian.
Familiar form: Nzhtig (Նժդիկ).

O

Oksen — Օգսէն
A Greek name of unknown origin.

Onnig — Օննիկ
'Little John,' from Hovhannes (Յովհաննէս).
Onnik Derdzakian (pen name Vramian; 1871-1915),
Armenian international writer, editor, and politician based in Turkey.

Oshin — Օշին
'Thyme,' from the Persian.
Oshin, ancestor of the medieval Hetumid dynasty of Armenian Cilicia.

Ounan — Ունան
'Dove,' from the Hebrew.
An alternative form of Hovnan (Յովնան).

P

Pagour — Բակուր
Pagouran — Բակուրան
'Child of God,' from the Old Persian.

Pailag — Փայլակ
'Lightning,' from the Armenian.
Pailag (real name Hagop Baronian; 1843-1891), writer, commentator, and satirist.

Pakarad — Բագարատ
'Gift of God,' from Old Persian.
Alternative forms: **Pako** (Բագո), and **Pakos** (Բագոս).

Palasan — Բալասան
'Balsam,' from the Armenian.
Alternative forms: **Pala** (Բալա), **Palas** (Բալաս), and **Palo** (Բալո).

Palig — Բալիկ
'Little child,' from the Armenian *pala* 'kid.'

Panos — Փանոս
'Shining one,' from the Greek *panos* 'shining.'
Familiar form: **Panig** (Փանիկ).

Pap — Բապ
'Father,' or 'grandfather,' from the Persian.
Familiar forms: **Papi** (Բապի), and **Papig** (Բապիկ).

Papel — Բաբէլ
'From the tribe of Babylon,' from the Hebrew.

Paramaz — Փարամազ
'Governor,' from the Persian.

107

Paranem — Փառանեմ
An Ancient Persian name of unknown origin.

Paren — Փառէն
'Glory,' from the Persian.

Parnag — Փառնակ
'Glorious arm,' from the Persian.

Parounag — Բարունակ
'Grape vine,' from the Armenian.

Parsegh — Բարսեղ
'King,' from the Greek.
*Parsegh Varaketsi, 16th-century priest and chronicler of the
Turco-Persian wars over the territories of Armenia.*

Partam — Փարթամ
'Wealthy,' from the Armenian.

Partogh — Բարթող
'Child of God,' from the Hebrew.

Patig — Բաթիկ
'Little duck,' from the Armenian *pat* 'duck.'

Pavsdos — Փաւստոս
'Happy,' from the Greek.
Pavsdos Puzantatsi, chronicler of Armenian history who lived in the 4th-5th centuries.

Pazé — Բազէ
'Hawk,' from the Armenian.

Pazoug — Բազուկ
'Strong-arm,' from the Armenian.

Pegor — Բեկոր
'Little one,' from the Armenian.

Peklar — Բեգլար
'Princes,' from the Ottoman Turkish *beg*.

Peniamin — Բենիամին
'Fortunate,' from the Hebrew 'son of the right hand.'
The Armenian form of **Benjamin**.
Familiar form: **Penig** (Բենիկ).

Pertag — Բերդակ
'Little citadel,' from the Armenian *pert*.

Petros — Պետրոս
'Rock,' from the Greek *petros*.
An Armenian form of **Peter**.
Pedro Petrossian, *Brazilian politician, and governor of
the state of Mato Grosso.*

Pilibbos — Փիլիպպոս
Pilibos — Փիլիպոս
'Lover of horses,' from the Greek *philos* 'friend,'
and *hippos* 'horse.'
The Armenian form of **Philip**.
Alternative forms: **Philip** (Ֆիլիփ), **Pilippé** (Փիլիփէ),
Pilig (Փիլիկ), and **Pilo** (Փիլo).

Pouys — Բnյս
'Potent herb,' from the Armenian.

Punig — Փիւնիկ
'Phoenix,' from the Armenian.

Purad — Բիւրատ
An ancient name of unknown origin.

Puzant — Բիւզանդ
'Byzantine man,' from the Armenian.

R

Rafayel — Ռաֆայէլ
'Healed by God,' from the Hebrew *rapha* 'to heal,' and *El* 'God.'
The Armenian form of **Raphael**.

Raffi/Rafi — Ռաֆֆի/Րաֆֆի
Rafig — Ռաֆիկ
'Glorious man,' from the Arabic.
Raffi (real name Hagop Melik Hagopian; 1835-1888),
Armenian historical novelist.
Raffi (Cavoukian) (1948-), Egypt-born Canadian singer, songwriter, author,
and children's entertainer.

Razmig — Ռազմիկ
'Warrior,' from the Armenian.

Reteos — Ռեթէոս
'Divine,' from the Greek.
Alternative forms: **Ratevos** (Ռաթեւոս),
and **Retevos** (Ռեթեւոս).
Familiar form: **Retig** (Ռեթիկ).

Robert — Ռոբերտ
'Man of brilliant reputation,' from the Teutonic.
Robert Zildjian (1923-), developer of the world famous Zildjian
and Sabian cymbals.

Roland — Ռոլանդ
'From the famed land,' from the Teutonic.

Romanos — Ռոմանոս
'Great strength,' from the Greek.

Rosdom — Ռոստոմ
'Torrent,' from the Ancient Persian.

Roupen — Ռուբէն
'Behold a son,' from the Hebrew.
Familiar form: **Roupig** (Ռուբիկ).
Rouben Mamoulian (1897-1987), award-winning Hollywood stage/cinema director, writer, and producer. His movies include 'Dr. Jekyll and Mr. Hyde' and 'The Mask of Zorro.'

Rshdouni — Ռշտունի
The name of a famous Armenian princely dynasty.

S

Saghatel — Սաղաթէլ
'God's wish,' from the Hebrew.

Sahag — Սահակ
'The one who makes God smile,' from the Hebrew *Yitzhaq*.
An Armenian form of **Isaac**.
Saint Sahag Ardzronig (?-786) and **Saint Sahag Garnetsig** (?-808), aristocrats, revolutionaries, and martyrs.
Bishop Sahag (?-454), saint and martyr.
Catholicos Sahag Bartev (348-437), saint, first translator of the Holy Bible into Armenian, and the guiding force of Armenia's Golden Age.

Sam — Սամ
'Fiery rainbow,' from the Persian.

Samson — Սամսոն
'Man of the son,' from the Hebrew.

Samuel — Սամուէլ
'Heard by God,' from the Hebrew.
Familiar forms: **Sam** (Սամ), **Samig** (Սամիկ), and **Samo** (Սամo).

Santour — Սանթուր
'Lute,' from the Armenian.

Sarhad — Սարհատ
'Frontier,' from the Persian.

Saripek — Սարիբէգ
'Fair lord,' from the Ottoman Turkish.

Sarkis — Սարգիս
'Rainbow,' from the Persian or Assyrian.
Alternative forms: **Sarki** (Սարգի), and **Sarko** (Սարգո).
Familiar form: **Saki** (Սագի).
Sargis Sargsian (1973-), Armenian–U.S. champion tennis player.
*Sarkis is also found in the family name of **Cher** (Cherilyn Sarkissian; 1946-),*
U.S. singer, and Oscar-winning film actress.

Saro — Սարո
'Cypress tree,' from the Armenian.
William Saroyan (1908-1981), U.S. novelist and playwright, who won the Pulitzer Prize
for his stage play 'The Time of Your Life.'

Sashipeg — Սաշիբեկ
A name of unknown origin from the Ottoman Turkish.

Sasoun — Սասուն
The name of an Armenian town and province.

Satoun — Սատուն
An ancient name of unknown origin, used by princes of the
Ardzrouni family in the 12th-13th centuries.

Sayat — Սայաթ
'Hunter,' from the Arabic *sayyad*.
Sayat Nova (Haroutioun Sayatian; 1712-1795), renowned bard ('ashoug' or 'kousan')
and songwriter who traveled and worked throughout the Caucasus.

Sdepan — Ստեփան
'Crowned one,' from the Greek *stephanos*.
The Armenian form of **Stephen**.
Alternative forms: **Depan** (Տեփան), **Depo** (Տեփո), **Depig** (Տեփիկ),
Sdep (Ստեփ), **Sdepané** (Ստեփանէ), and **Sepan** (Սեփան).
*Stepan Shahumian (1878-1918), influential Bolshevik revolutionary leader,
and one of the 26 People's Commissars executed in 1918.*

Sebouh — Սեպուհ
'Knight,' from the Armenian.

Seghpos — Սեղբոս
'Son of the forest,' from the Greek.

Seno — Սենօ
'Moon god,' from the Ancient Assyrian.
Familiar forms: **Sen** (Սէն), and **Senig** (Սենիկ).

Sergei — Սերգեյ
'Guardian,' from the Latin.
*Sergei Paradjanov (1924-1990), Armenian artist and moviemaker from Georgia, whose
most famous movie is 'The Color of Pomegranates.'*

Sero — Սերօ
Serop — Սերոբ
'Angel,' from the Armenian *serovpe* 'seraph.'

Seryozha — Սերյոժա
An ancient Russian origin of unknown meaning.

Seth — Սեթ
'God's appointed one,' from the Hebrew.

Setrag — Սեդրակ
Setrak — Սեդրաք
An ancient name of Babylonian origin.

Sevag — Սեւակ
'Dark eyes,' from the Armenian.

Sevan — Սեւան
The name of a lake in Armenia.

Sevig — Սեւիկ
'Little dark one,' from the Armenian *sev* 'black.'

Seyran — Սէյրան
'Man of leisure,' from the Arabic.

Shabouh — Շապուհ
'Son of the king,' from the Pahlavi.

Shadarev — Շատարեւ
'Long-lived,' from the Armenian.

Shahan — Շահան
'King of kings,' from the Persian *Shahanshah*.
Shahan Shanour (real name Shahnour Kerestejian; 1903-1974), author based in France.

Shahé — Շահէ
'King,' from the Persian.

Shahen — Շահէն
'Falcon,' from the Pahlavi.
Familiar form: Shahig (Շահիկ).

Shahnour — Շահնուր
'Fire king,' from the Persian/Armenian *shah* 'king,' and *nour* 'fire.'
Charles Aznavour (real name Shahnour Aznavourian; 1924-), French international singer and songwriter.

Shakar — Շաքար
'Sugar,' from the Armenian.

Shant — Շանթ
'Lightning,' from the Armenian.

Shara — Շարա
'Full of eagerness,' from the Persian.

Shavarsh — Շավարշ
Shavasb — Շավասպ
'Master of the black stallion,' from the Persian.

Sheg — Շեկ
'Auburn,' from the Armenian.
Familiar form: **Shego** (Շեկո).

Shen — Շեն
'Cheerful,' from the Armenian.

Sheram — Շերամ
'Silkworm,' from the Armenian.

Shirag — Շիրակ
The name of a region in Armenia.

Shiraz — Շիրազ
'Free as a lion,' from the Persian Shirazabad.

Shirvan — Շիրվան
'Keeper of lions,' from the Persian.

Shmavon — Շմավոն
'Loyal,' from the Hebrew.

Shnork — Շնորհք
'Talented and graceful,' from the Armenian.

Simeon — Սիմէոն
'God has granted,' or 'snub-nosed,' both from the Hebrew.
Saint Simeon (?-604), one of the hermit martyrs called the Seven Witnesses.

115

Simon — Սիմոն
'Granter of wishes,' from the Hebrew.
Simon Vratsian (real name Simavon Gruzian; 1882-1969),
Armenian international writer, editor, and politician.

Simpad — Սմբատ
An ancient name of unknown origin.

Sinan — Սինան
'Lance,' from the Arabic.

Sion — Սիոն
'Watch tower,' from the Hebrew.

Sipan — Սիփան
The name of a mountain in Armenia.

Siragan — Սիրական
'Handsome to the eye,' from the Armenian.
Alternative form: **Siregan** (Սիրեկան).
Familiar form: **Sirag** (Սիրակ).

Sisag — Սիսակ
'Prince's palace,' from the Armenian.

Sisé — Սիսէ
An ancient name of unknown origin

Slak — Սլաք
'Arrow,' from the Armenian.

Soghomon — Սողոմոն
'Peaceful one,' from the Hebrew.
Alternative forms: **Soghig** (Սողիկ), **Sogho** (Սողո), **Soghom** (Սողոմ),
and **Soughi** (Սուղի).
Soghomon Soghomonian (Gomidas [Komitas] Vartabed; 1869-1935),
pioneering musicologist of Armenian church and folk music.

Soukias — Սուքիաս
'Calm,' from the Greek.

Souren — Սուրէն
'Powerful' from the Pahlavi.
Familiar forms: **Sorig** (Սորիկ), **Sourig** (Սուրիկ),
and **Souro** (Սուրo).

Spartion — Սպարթիոն
Ancient name of unknown origin,
derived perhaps from the Greek city of Sparta.

Stephan — Ստեփան
An alternative form of **Sdepan** (Ստտփան).
*Steven Zaillian (1951-), Oscar award-winning screenwriter of films such as
'Schindler's List,' 'Patriot Games,' 'Awakenings,' and 'Hannibal.'*

Svin — Սուին
'Dagger,' from the Armenian.

Տ

Takavor — Թագաւոր
Takvor — Թագւոր
'King,' from the Armenian.

Taniel — Դանիէլ
An alternative form of **Daniel** (Տանիէլ).

Tarman — Դարման
'Healer,' from the Armenian.

117

Tat — Թաթ
'Paw,' from the Armenian.
Familiar form: Tatig (Թաթիկ).
Bishop Tatig (?-454), saint and martyr.

Tateos — Թադէոս
'Wise,' from the Assyrian.
Alternative forms: Tatevos (Թադեւոս),
Tatos (Թադոս), and Tevos (Թեւոս).
Familiar forms: Tate (Թաթէ), and Tato (Թաթո).

Tatoul — Թաթուլ
'Little paw,' from the Armenian.
Saint Tatoul, fifth-century hermit.
Tatoul Altounian (1901-1973), musician, choreographer, and director of Armenia's national folk song and dance ensemble.

Tavit — Դաւիթ
'Beloved one,' from Hebrew.
Alternative forms: Tavtag (Թաւդակ), and Tavo (Դաւo)
Saint Tavit the Invincible, fifth-century philosopher and one of the Holy Translators.
Saint Tavit Tvinetsi (?-701), general and martyr.

Teotoros — Թէոդորոս
Teotos — Թէոդոս
'Gift from God,' from the Greek. The Armenian form of **Theodore**.
Familiar forms: Torig (Թորիկ), and Totig (Թոդիկ).
Prince Teotoros, 12th-century monk, saint, and martyr.

Terenig — Դերենիկ
'Little pilgrim,' from the Armenian.

Tev — Թեւ
'Strong arm,' from the Armenian.
Familiar form: Tevig (Թեւիկ).

Tigran — Տիգրան
An alternative form of **Dikran** (Տիգրան).
Tigran Petrossian (1929-1984), Armenian world chess champion.

Torkom — Թորգոմ
'Steadfast one,' from the Hebrew.

Tornig — Թոռնիկ
'Grandson,' from the Armenian.
Tornig Mamigonian (?-1073), prince of Sassoun who defeated the Turks.

Toukhair — Թուխայր
Toukhig — Թուխիկ
'Dark one,' from the Armenian *toukh* 'brown.'

Tourig — Թուրիկ
'Little sword,' from the Armenian *tour* 'sword.'

Tovmas — Թովմաս
'Doubter,' from the Greek. The Armenian form of **Thomas**.
Alternative form: **Tovma** (Թովմա).
Familiar form: **Tovig** (Թովիկ).
Saint Tovmas, fifth-century monk.

Trasdamad — Դրաստամատ
'One who never goes astray,' from the Pahlavi.
Alternative form: **Tro** (Դրո).

Tsakig — Ձագիկ
'Young one,' from the Armenian.

Tsavag — Ցավակ
'Eye-ache,' from the Armenian.

Tsolag — Ցոլակ
'Bright eyes,' from the Armenian.

Tvin — Դուին
The name of an ancient capital of Armenia.

Ս

Undza — Ընձա
'Gift,' from the Armenian.

Untsag — Ընծակ
'Tiger cub,' from the Armenian.

Uzkon — Զգոն
'Wise one,' from the Armenian.

Վ

Vagharsh — Վաղարշ
Vagharshag — Վաղարշակ
'Valakhs,' from the Pahlavi.
Alternative form: **Vaghoush** (Վաղուշ).
Familiar form: **Vagho** (Վաղո).

Vaghinag — Վաղինակ
An ancient name of unknown origin.

Vahak — Վահագ
Vahakn — Վահագն
The god of war in ancient Armenian mythology.

Vahan — Վահան
'Shield,' derived from the name of the Armenian god Vahagn.
Familiar forms: **Vahanig** (Վահանիկ), and **Vahig** (Վահիկ).
Saint Vahan Koghnatsi *(?-737), patriot and martyr.*
Vahan Tekeyan *(1878-1945), Armenian literary and political figure.*

120

Vahé — Վահէ
'Best,' from the Ancient Persian.

Vahram — Վահրամ
'Spring,' from the Pahlavi, and the name of the god
of the planet Mars.

Vahrij — Վահրիճ
'Bounty that flows,' from the Pahlavi.

Van — Վան
The name of a town and lake in Western Armenia.
Familiar forms: **Vani** (Վանի), **Vano** (Վանo),
and **Vanoush** (Վանուշ).

Vanadour — Վանատուր
'Gift of the monastery,' from the Armenian.

Vanagan — Վանական
'Belonging to the monastery,' from the Armenian.

Varak — Վարագ
Name of the famous monastery of Varak and its mountain.

Varant — Վարանդ
From the name of the Armenian princedom,
or melikdom, of Varanta.

Varaz — Վարազ
'Wild boar,' from the Persian.
Varaztad Kazanjian, U.S. physician, known as the 'Father of Plastic Surgery.'

Varoujan — Վարուժան
'Dove,' from the Armenian.
Familiar forms: **Varouj/Varouzh** (Վարուժ).

121

Varsag — Վարսակ
Varsig — Վարսիկ
'Hairy' from the Armenian *vars* 'hair.'

Varsham — Վարշամ
'Lord,' from the Babylonian.

Vart — Վարդ
'Rose,' from the Armenian.
Alternative form: **Vardo** (Վարդո).

Vartan — Վարդան
An ancient name of Iranian origin.

Varteni, the baptismal name of **Saint Shoushan** (?-470), saint and martyr.
Saint Vartan Mamigonian (?-451), general and martyr.
Vartan Gregorian (1926-), educationalist whose appointments include President of the Carnegie Foundation, Head of N.Y. Public Library, and President of of Brown University.

Vartavar — Վարդավառ
'Feast of the Transfiguration,' from the Armenian.

Vartazad — Վարդազադ
'Free as a rose,' from the Armenian.

Varter — Վարդեր
'Roses,' from the Armenian *vart*.

Varteres — Վարդերես
'Rosy cheeked,' from the Armenian.

Vartkes — Վարդգես
'Redhead,' from the Armenian.

Vasag — Վասակ
'Independent,' from the Persian.

122

Vashdag — Վաշտակ
'Regiment,' from the Armenian *vashd*.

Vatchag — Վաչակ
Vatchagan — Վաչական
Vatché — Վաչէ
'Boy,' from the Ancient Persian.
Familiar form: **Vatchig** (Վաչիկ).

Vazken — Վազգէն
'Frog,' from the Old and Middle Persian.
Familiar form: **Vazo** (Վազo).

Vem — Վէմ
'Rock,' from the Armenian.

Viken — Վիգէն
Viktor — Վիկտոր
Vitchen — Վիչէն
'Victorious one,' from the Latin *victor*.
Viktor Hambartsumian, Armenian astrophysicist and theoretician.
Victor Maghakian (1921-1977), one of the most decorated American soldiers of the Second World War.

Vladimir — Վլադիմիր
'Great ruler,' from the Slavic.

Voki — Ոգի
'Spirit,' from the Armenian.

Vosdan — Ոստան
'Citadel,' from the Armenian.
Familiar form: **Vosdanig** (Ոստանիկ).
Arshile Gorky (real name Vostanik-Manuk Adayan; 1904-1948), U.S. abstract painter.

Vosgan — Ոսկան
'Gold,' from the Armenian.

Vosgeperan — Ոսկեբերան
'Golden-tongued,' from the Armenian.

Vosgetar — Ոսկեդար
'Golden Age,' from the Armenian.

Vosgi — Ոսկի
'Gold,' from the Armenian.

Saint Vosgi (?-107), one of the first Armenian converts and martyrs.

Vram — Վռամ
'Fiery,' from the Persian *bahram*.

Vran — Վրան
'Tabernacle,' from the Armenian.

Vrej/Vrezh — Վրէժ
'Vengeance,' from the Armenian.

Vren — Վրէն
'Manly,' from the Persian.

Vrouyr — Վրույր
An ancient name of unknown origin.

Vrtanes — Վրթանէս
An ancient name of unknown origin.

Vshdig — Վշտիկ
'Little anguish,' from the Armenian *vishd*.

Կ

Yeghia –– Եղիա
'Jehovah is my God,' from the Hebrew.
Familiar forms: **Eghig** (Էղիկ), **Yeghi** (Եղի),
Yeghig (Եղիկ), and **Yegho** (Եղո).

Yeghiazar — Եղիազար
'God is my helper,' from the Hebrew.

Yeghishé — Եղիշէ
'God is my salvation,' from the Hebrew.
Familiar form: **Yeghish** (Եղիշ).
Saint Yeghishé, fifth-century historian, and one of the Holy Translators.
*Yeghishé Charents (1897-1937), Armenian writer and poet who was also the translator
of the works of Gorky, Goethe, and Pushkin.*

Yeghivart — Եղիվարդ
'Preacher,' from the Armenian.

Yeghvart — Եղվարդ
'Rose oil,' from the Armenian *yegh* 'oil,' and *vart* 'rose.'

Yenok —Ենովք
'Devoted,' from the Hebrew.

Yeprad — Եփրատ
From the name of one of the rivers of Armenia.

Yeprem — Եփրեմ
'Fruitful,' or 'faithful,' from the Hebrew.

Yeram — Երամ
'Flock of birds,' from the Armenian.

125

Yeraz — Երազ
'Dream,' from the Armenian.

Yerchanig — Երջանիկ
'Lucky,' from the Armenian.
Alternative form: **Yerchan** (Երջան).

Yeremia — Երեմիա
'Abandoned,' from the Hebrew. The Armenian form of **Jeremiah**.
Alternative form: **Yerem** (Երեմ).

Yerevan — Երեւան
From the name of the capital of the Republic of Armenia.

Yergat — Երկաթ
'Steel,' from the Armenian.

Yertik — Երդիկ
'Roof-top,' from the Armenian.

Yervant — Երվանդ
'Energetic one,' from the Pahlavi.
Yervant Kochar (1899-1979), painter and sculptor who created the famous equestrian statue of David of Sassoun in Yerevan.

Yessai — Եսայի
'Salvation of God,' from the Hebrew.
Alternative form: **Yesso** (Եսսո).

Yetvart — Եդուարդ
'Guardian of the treasury,' from the Anglo-Saxon *ead* 'treasure,' and *ward* 'keeper.' The Armenian form of **Edward**.

Yeznig — Եզնիկ
'Little bull,' from the Armenian.
Yeznig Goghpatsi, fifth-century philosopher and cleric who translated the Bible into Armenian.

Youri — Յուրի
'Farmer,' from the Russian form of the Greek **Giorgos** or **George**.
Youri Djorkaeff (1968-), French international soccer player and member of
France's 1998 World Cup winning team.

Youssouf — Յուսուֆ
An alternative form of **Yovseb**.
Youssouf Karsh (1908-), Turkish-born Canadian celebrity photographer
and genius of the modern image.

Yovsep — Յովսեփ
'May God send more children,' from the Hebrew *Yosefyah*.
An Armenian form of **Joseph**.

Z

Zadig — Զատիկ
'Resurrection,' or 'Easter,' from the Armenian.

Zakar — Զաքար
Zakaria — Զաքարիա
'Memory of God,' from the Hebrew.
Familiar form: Zako (Զաքո).
Zakaria Yergaynapazug (?-1214), prince of Ani, and commander
of the royal army of Georgia.

Zaré — Զարէ
'Tears,' from the Persian *zareh*.
Zaré, the king who, in the second century B.C., liberated Armenia
from the Seleucid Empire.
Zaré Vorpouni (1903-1980), influential writer and thinker based in France.
Zaré Moutafian (1907-1980), painter based in France.

Zarevant — Զարեւանդ
The name of a region of Armenia.

Zarkoun — Զարգուն
'Youthful,' from the Armenian.

Zarl — Զարլ
An ancient name of unknown origin.

Zarmair/Zarmayr — Զարմայր
'Hero,' from the Armenian.
Familiar forms: **Zarmig** (Զարմիկ), and **Zarmo** (Զարմո).

Zaven — Զաւէն
'Helper,' from the Persian.
Familiar form: **Zavig** (Զաւիկ).

Zhirair — Ժիրայր
'Agile,' from the Armenian.
Familiar forms: **Zhirig** (Ժիրիկ), and **Zhiro** (Ժիրո).

Zohrab — Զոհրապ
'Flaming red,' from the Arabic/Persian name for the planet Venus.

Zorair/Zorayr — Զորայր
'Strong man,' from the Armenian/Persian.

Zoravar — Զորավար
'General,' from the Armenian.
Familiar form: **Zora** (Զորա), **Zori** (Զորի), and **Zorig** (Զորիկ).

Zoulal — Զուլալ
'Crystal clear,' from the Armenian.